SCOTTISH CIVIC

HERALDRY

Regional – Islands – District

By the same Author:

SCOTTISH BURGH AND COUNTY HERALDRY, 1973

Scottish Civic Heraldry

Regional – Islands – District

by

R. M. URQUHART

HERALDRY TODAY
10 Beauchamp Place, London, S.W.3

I.S.B.N. 0 90045526 8

Photoset, printed and bound
in Great Britain by
Redwood Burn Ltd
Trowbridge & Esher

FOR
MHOIRE AND LESLEY

CONTENTS

FOREWORD

by Sir James Monteith Grant, K.C.V.O., W.S., Lord Lyon King of Arms

This book from Mr. R. M. Urquhart's able and scholarly pen deals with the armorial bearings granted to the new statutory Local Authorities in Scotland. It follows the general pattern of his very successful *Scottish Burgh and County Heraldry*. It contains illustrations of all the new Coats of Arms with the author's commentary on each in his usual interesting and informative style and is prefaced by a full and very instructive introduction. Mr. Urquhart has kindly invited me to write a Foreword to this new book and it has given me much pleasure to do so.

The Local Government (Scotland) Act 1973 provided that on 16th May 1975 all Local Government areas in Scotland should cease to exist and should be replaced by the Regions, Islands Areas and Districts specified in the first Schedule of the Statute. The armorial bearings of the former Local Authorities, some of which were of great antiquity, likewise passed out of use on the appointed day and became little more than museum pieces.

It was necessary for all the new statutory bodies who desired to have armorial bearings to lodge appropriate Petitions with the Court of the Lord Lyon. They were so informed and nearly all of them have complied.

For Lyon it was a time of pressure and challenge because, as is perhaps not widely known, he alone is responsible for the form and design of all new armorial bearings which enter Lyon Register during his term of office. It is on these that posterity will judge him!

How the task was approached and the manner of its accomplishment is told in this beautifully produced and illustrated new book. I commend it warmly and wish it well.

J. MONTEITH GRANT
Lyon

AUTHOR'S NOTE

Now that the position regarding the heraldry of the new Local Authorities in Scotland has been virtually finalised, it has seemed appropriate to bring up-to-date the record started with *Scottish Burgh and County Heraldry* in 1973.

I am most grateful to the Lord Lyon King of Arms, Sir James Monteith Grant, for his kindness in writing the Foreword and for the interest he has shown in my work during my visits to the Lyon Office where I have been shown the greatest consideration and given every assistance. I wish to thank particularly Mr. Malcolm Innes of Edingight, Lyon Clerk and Marchmont Herald, for allowing me access to the case files and for much help and advice, and also Miss Susan Pomphrey, who has regularly kept me informed as the grants have been approved and who has so readily answered my postal queries.

I would like to express my most sincere thanks to Miss Jennifer Mitchell, Herald Painter to the Court of the Lord Lyon, who did the drawings for me to such a high standard of excellence and was also of great general assistance to me.

I am also grateful to the members of the Scottish Development Department for providing information about the Reform of Local Government in Scotland; to Mr. Alan Burn of the University of Southampton Cartographic Unit and his staff for the preparation of the map of Scotland; to Miss Wendy Spashett for her help with the typing of the manuscript; and to the many others who have provided information and assistance.

Southampton
1979

PART I

The New Councils
and their Heraldry

1. Reform and Change

On 16 May 1975 the Local Government (Scotland) Act 1973 (Eliz. II 1973 chapter 65) came into force and the whole structure and pattern of local government in Scotland was changed. The thirty-three county councils, the two hundred and one burghs (including the four counties of cities) and their town councils, and the one hundred and ninety-seven district councils, details of which I have set out in Appendix I, were swept away. In their place came nine Regional Councils, three Islands Councils, and fifty-three District Councils.

This great change had stemmed from the publication in September 1969 of the *Report of the Royal Commission on Local Government in Scotland 1966–69* (Cmnd. 4150), whose Chairman was Lord Wheatley, the Lord Justice Clerk. Finding that the structure of Scottish local government was no longer adequate to cope with present-day needs, the Royal Commission recommended that in future Scotland should be administered by a two-tier system of local government consisting of seven Regional Authorities and thirty-seven District Authorities made up as follows:

Region	*Comprising Counties of*
Highlands & Islands (8 Districts)	Zetland, Orkney, Caithness, Sutherland, Ross & Cromarty, Inverness, Nairn, Moray (southern end), Banff (south-western end), Argyll (except south-eastern part).
North-East (4 Districts)	Moray (except southern end), Banff (except south-western end), Aberdeen, City of Aberdeen, Kincardine (northern half).
East (4 Districts)	Kincardine (southern half), Angus, City of Dundee, Perth (except south-western part and small part in south), Kinross, Fife (northern half).
South-East (6 Districts)	Fife (southern half, except for south-western corner), East Lothian, Midlothian, City of Edinburgh, West Lothian (except north-western part), Peebles, Selkirk, Roxburgh (except south-western end), Berwick.
Central (2 Districts)	Perth (south-western part and small part in south), Stirling (except south-western part), Clackmannan, Fife (south-western corner), West Lothian (north-western part).

Region	Comprising Counties of
West (11 Districts)	Argyll (south-eastern part), Bute, Dunbarton, Stirling (south-western part), Lanark, City of Glasgow, Renfrew, Ayr.
South-West (2 Districts)	Wigtown, Kirkcudbright, Dumfries, Roxburgh (south-western end).

The Regional Authorities would form the first tier and have responsibility for major services; at second-tier level, the District Authorities would take charge of a wide range of local services. At a more local level, there would be Community Councils, but they would exercise no statutory functions.

As might be expected, the Report caused much discussion and controversy. Almost 400 comments were sent in to the Scottish Office by existing local authorities, organisations and individuals. Particular points of objection raised were the splitting of the county of Fife between the East and South-East Regions, the absence of a separate Region for the Borders, the vast size of the West Region, and the lack of consideration for the special position of Shetland, Orkney and the Western Isles. There was also criticism of the large size of many of the Districts and support for an increase in their number; there were many suggestions for boundary adjustments.

In February 1971, the Government issued its views on the Report in a White Paper entitled *Reform of Local Government in Scotland* (Cmnd. 4583). While acknowledging the great value of the Report, the Government did not accept all its recommendations but considered that it provided a foundation on which the new system could be built. The Government's proposals envisaged eight Regional Authorities, two Islands Authorities and forty-nine District Authorities on these lines:

Regions
Highlands (10 Districts), North-East (5 Districts), East (4 Districts), South-East (6 Districts), Borders (4 Districts), Central (3 Districts), West (13 Districts), South-West (4 Districts).

Islands Areas
Shetland, Orkney.

The new plan included nearly all of Argyll in the West Region which thus became even larger, although it lost part of South-West Ayrshire to South-West. The whole of Kincardineshire went to North-East. Fife remained divided between East and South-East, and the latter yielded some territory to the new Borders Region. The Highlands and Islands Region, as well as losing the greater part of Argyll, lost Shetland and Orkney, but kept Western Isles; it was renamed Highlands.

The White Paper also set out firm proposals about the functions of the new Authorities. The Regional Authorities were to deal with major planning and related services, education, social work, regional housing, police, fire, coast protection, consumer protection, weights & measures and food standards, diseases of animals, community centres*, parks and recreation*, museums and art galleries*, registrations of births deaths and marriages, registration of electors. The District Authorities were to cover local planning and associated services†, building control†, housing, community centres*, parks and recreation*, museums and art galleries*, libraries†, environmental health, regulation and licensing of cinemas, theatres, betting and gaming, taxis, etc. In Highlands, Borders and South-West Regions, the functions marked † would be Regional; functions marked * would be exercised concurrently by Regional and District Authorities. Islands Authorities were to be given virtually the same functions as Regional Authorities, though the police and fire arrangements (already on an area basis) had to be similar to those at present in force.

These proposals by the Government provoked further debate and, in December 1971, following discussions with local authority associations, the Secretary of State made a Parliamentary Statement[1] in which he announced some changes in the conclusions of the White Paper. Islands Authority status was granted to the Western Isles (Lewis, Harris, the Uists and Barra) and the Highland Region was reduced accordingly; six adjustments were made to Regional boundaries and nineteen to District boundaries; Regional Authorities were given responsibility for water, sewerage and river purification, and for harbours controlled by existing local authorities.

The following month the Scottish Office sent SDD Circular No. 4/1972 to all local authorities announcing the above-mentioned boundary changes and giving for comment a list of the suggested names for the new Authorities. When replies had been received and considered, SDD Circular No. 65/1972 was issued in July 1972 giving the names of the new Authorities to be included in the Bill.

But the discussion was not yet over. There were many tussles during the debates on the Bill in both Houses of Parliament[2], during which the Government accepted several amendments which made changes to the proposed structure. Fife received its desired Regional status and the reduced Forth (South-East) Region was re-named Lothian. The Strathclyde (West) Region survived all attempts to split it up and, in the end, was increased by the transfer to it of South-West Ayrshire from the Dumfries & Galloway (South-West) Region, but the number of Districts in it was increased from thirteen to nineteen, four being split off from the proposed Glasgow District and a further two being made in Ayrshire. Some minor boundary changes were made in certain Regions and Districts and one or two changes in the names of Districts were approved. The Bill received the Royal Assent on 25 October 1973 and "the appointed day" for the change-over was fixed at 16 May 1975.

The structure of local government for Scotland approved in the Act provides for nine Regions, three Islands Areas, and fifty-three Districts as summarised below:

Region	*Comprising Counties of*
Highland (8 Districts)	Caithness, Sutherland, Ross & Cromarty (except Lewis), Inverness (except Harris, the Uists and Barra), Nairn, Moray (southern end), Argyll (northern end).

Region	*Comprising Counties of*
Grampian (5 Districts)	Moray (except southern end), Banff, Aberdeen, City of Aberdeen, Kincardine.
Tayside (3 Districts)	Angus, City of Dundee, Perth (except south-western part), Kinross.
Fife (3 Districts)	Fife.
Lothian (4 Districts)	East Lothian, Midlothian (except south-eastern end), City of Edinburgh, West Lothian (except north-western corner).
Central (3 Districts)	Perth (south-western part), Stirling (except south-western part), Clackmannan, West Lothian (north-western corner).
Borders (4 Districts)	Midlothian (south-eastern end), Peebles, Selkirk, Roxburgh, Berwick.
Strathclyde (19 Districts)	Argyll (except northern end), Bute, Dunbarton, Stirling (south-western part), Lanark, City of Glasgow, Renfrew, Ayr.
Dumfries & Galloway (4 Districts)	Wigtown, Kirkcudbright, Dumfries.

Islands Area	*Comprising Counties of*
Orkney	Orkney.
Shetland	Zetland.
Western Isles	Ross & Cromarty (Lewis), Inverness (Harris, the Uists and Barra).

Fuller details are given in the individual articles in Part II and in the map at the end of the book.

Each Region, Islands Area, and District has its own Council. These Councils are Scotland's new Local Authorities.

The Act required each Islands Council and District Council to submit to the Secretary of State a scheme for the establishment of Community Councils for its area. A Community Council is not a local authority and is virtually wholly financially dependent on the Local Authorities for its area, i.e. Regional (or Islands) and District Council; its purpose is to ascertain and represent the views and opinions of its community to its Local Authorities, and "to take such action in the interests of that community as appears to be reasonable and practicable". The overall scheme for Community Councils is now virtually complete, and it is possible that there could eventually be some thirteen hundred of them.

2. The Lord Lyon and the New Councils

As can be seen from Appendix I, one hundred and seventy-eight burghs, and all the thirty-three county councils, had received grants of arms. These are described in *Scottish Burgh and County Heraldry* (published 1973) except for the Burgh of Doune which did not register arms until 1974. Details are given in Appendix II along with a description of the arms of the two armigerous (old) district councils, Arran and Gairloch.

It had, however, taken just over 300 years to achieve the position on the burghs and even in 1975, there were still three cases of burghs illegally using armorial bearings.[3] And so the Lyon Office made careful plans to deal with grants of arms to the new Local Authorities in a systematic way.

As the powers of the Lord Lyon were derived from an Act of the Scottish Parliament passed in 1672 (1672, c.21; fol. edit. c.47 (Car. II) "Concerning the Privileges of the Office of Lyon King-at-Arms"), concern was felt lest new Councils created in 1975 should consider that an Act, which was 303 years old, was hardly relevant to their situation. A suggestion was, therefore, made that a clause should be included in the Local Government (Scotland) Bill reminding the new Councils that, if they wished to have and use armorial bearings, application for these must be made in proper form to the Court of the Lord Lyon. This was duly considered, and an amendment on these lines was moved by the Earl of Balfour during the debate on the Bill in the House of Lords on 17 July 1973. In reply on behalf of the Government, Lord Drumalbyn said that Lord Balfour had done a service in bringing up the matter so that the new Local Authorities would be in no doubt whatsoever about the correct procedure for acquiring a grant of arms. But he added that the amendment was not strictly necessary and, in any case, it was possible for the Scottish Office to remind the new Councils of the correct procedure by issuing a departmental circular.[4]

When the issue of this circular came up some months later, the Scottish Office considered that it would be more appropriate if the Lord Lyon himself, with the prestige of his office, circulated the new Councils soon after the first elections had been held on 7 May 1974. And so in June 1974, the Lord Lyon (Sir James Monteith Grant) wrote to the nine Regional Councils and the three Islands Councils; in his letters he explained the correct procedure to be followed in making application for a grant of arms and he also indicated the nature of the armorial bearings he had in mind for them. These letters had considerable success, not only with the Councils to whom they were addressed, but they also evoked a very good response from the District Councils, of whom thirty-one had submitted Petitions or expressed interest by February 1975. In that month the Lord Lyon wrote to the other twenty-two District Councils and explained the correct procedure to them.

By the end of 1975, fifty-six of the sixty-five new Councils had submitted Petitions to the Lyon Court. At the time of writing, all the Regional Councils, except Strathclyde, and all the Islands Councils have sought and been granted armorial bearings; of the fifty-three District Councils, forty-nine have sought and have received grants and four have stated that they do not wish to register arms. Thus, since neither Strathclyde nor any of the four last-mentioned is using arms illegally, i.e. by having armorial seals or using emblems which can be regarded as heraldic, the matter of Scotland's New Civic Heraldry has been virtually settled and recorded in the Public Register of All Arms and Bearings in Scotland, where the first part of Volume 59 has been specially reserved for the purpose, thus renewing the practice followed when the Register was first started in 1672.[5]

Turning to the heraldry itself, it can be mentioned here that Lord Lyon Monteith Grant had decided that there were to be clear and precise rules to be followed in making grants of arms to the new Councils. These will be referred to as we go along, but one or two general matters should be noted now.

There was to be no question of the arms of an "old" authority passing as of right to one of the new Councils. Under Section 1(5) of the Act, all the old authorities conventionally died on 16 May 1975, and their armorial bearings consequently ceased to have an owner and reverted to the Crown, in the hands of the Lord Lyon who exercises the Royal Prerogative in these matters. It is of interest to mention here that a proposal to include in the Scottish Local Government Bill provision enabling the new Councils to inherit and continue to use the arms of their predecessors (as was done in the English Bill) was turned down as impracticable because of the form of the reorganisation in Scotland. It was considered that the best course was to let each new Council apply *de novo* in the normal way for a grant of arms. This, however, did not rule out the possibility, that where a new Council was responsible for roughly the same area as an old authority, a re-grant of the latter's arms, differenced as might be necessary, would be favourably considered.

The coats of arms for the new Councils were to be kept as simple as possible. The Regional Councils were to have a basic pattern to which suitable regional differences were to be added. As many of the Districts embraced several burghs and at least part of one county, it was necessary for these Councils to be selective in their choice of features to be included in their arms; otherwise it would be virtually impossible to produce a satisfactory achievement. This point was taken and so simplicity became and was accepted as the order of the day.

Since the new Councils had been created by Statute, their coats of arms were to be ensigned with specially devised coronets, thus continuing the practice first allowed in 1908 for the burghs by Lord Lyon Balfour Paul and introduced in 1951 by Lord Lyon Innes in relation to the county councils. Separate designs, each incorporating a thistle motif, were approved for Regional Councils and District Councils; the Regional coronet (as befitting a superior body) has leaved thistles, while the District coronet has thistle heads. Each Islands Council was given a coronet which has dolphins as the main feature. The coronets are gold in colour and more information about them is given below.

3. Arms for the Regional Councils

In devising armorial bearings for the REGIONAL COUNCILS, Lord Lyon Monteith Grant took due regard of the fact that they were all statutory creations which, as they came into being on the same day (16 May 1975), would rank *pari-passu*. He decided that their arms should in the main be the same, but that each should have two differences distinguishing it from all the others.

The Regional achievement consists of shield, supporters and coronet, but no motto. The shield has a basic design blazoned as follows:

Azure, a saltire Argent, surmounted at the fess point by an inescutcheon Gules, fimbriated Or, a bordure counter-compony of the First and Second.

In non-heraldic terms, the shield bears a silver St. Andrew's Cross on a blue field (to denote the Scottish identity) within a border of alternate blue and silver sections (to distinguish it from the Scottish national flag). At the middle of the cross is a small shield of red rimmed with gold, and on this is placed the *first* difference viz. an emblem or emblems associated with the Region.

The original Lyon Office suggestions for the Regional emblems were:— Highland (a star Argent); Grampian (a cross-crosslet fitchée Or); Tayside (a fleur-de-lis Argent); Fife (a dexter gauntlet apaumée Argent); Lothian (a sun in splendour Or); Central (a caltrap Or); Borders (a golden fleece); Strathclyde (an antique crown Argent); Dumfries & Galloway (a lion rampant Argent crowned Or). In the event these suggestions were varied in three instances: Tayside (a fleur-de-lis with a barrulet in chief Argent); Central (two caltraps in chief with a dexter gauntlet in base Or); Borders (four barrulets Argent between a salmon naiant in chief and a ram's head cabossed in base Proper). Then, as explained below, Fife was re-granted the former County Council arms, while the Strathclyde suggestion has not been implemented as the Regional Council has not yet applied for a grant of arms.

The case of Fife is of special interest. The Regional Council asked if it could be re-granted the arms (consisting of shield and motto) of Fife County Council since the Region had exactly the same boundaries as the former County and since it was the only Regional Council which could make such a claim. With characteristic understanding, Lord Lyon Monteith Grant allowed this request but insisted that supporters and coronet to the Regional pattern be added. Thus it can be said that Fife retains its old arms, including the Latin motto, and it is accordingly unique among the Regional Councils.

As to *Supporters*, Lyon's rules provided that in every case the sinister supporter to a Regional coat of arms should be a Scottish unicorn wearing a red collar with a saltire badge hanging from it. The dexter supporter was to be the *second* difference and would be chosen as something typical of, or closely related to, the particular Region.

The original Lyon Office scheme for the dexter supporters was:— Highland (a

Highland bull Proper); Grampian (a ptarmigan Proper); Tayside (an Angus Bull Proper); Fife (a horse Argent caparisoned Gules fimbriated Or); Lothian (a doe Proper); Central (a goshawk Proper); Borders (a black-faced ram Proper); Strathclyde (a Clydesdale stallion Proper); Dumfries & Galloway (a stag Proper). During the discussions with the Councils about the details of their arms, these changes were agreed:– Highland (a stag Or); Fife (St. Servanus Proper vested Argent); Lothian (a lion rampant Vert); Borders (a Border Knight Proper). The Strathclyde suggestion is still in suspense.

Each Regional coat of arms is ensigned with a coronet of leaved thistles in gold; the blazon is "a circlet richly chased from which are issuant four thistles leaved Or".

4.   Arms for the Islands Councils

It had originally been the intention that the ISLANDS COUNCILS should be granted achievements which would follow the Regional pattern with the following suggestions for emblem and dexter supporter:–

	Emblem	Dexter Supporter
Orkney	a Norse battle-axe in pale Or	a cock Proper
Shetland	a dragon ship, oars in action, Or	a Shetland pony Proper
Western Isles	a lymphad Or	a golden eagle Proper

This scheme was later abandoned in favour of one which allowed an individual design for the shield, supporters on the Regional pattern, a coronet, and a motto, if desired. Orkney was allowed to use on its shield the arms of the county council and to retain its motto. So was Shetland, which chose, however, to include a black raven for difference. Western Isles was granted a completely new coat of arms, with a Gaelic motto; in addition, at the request of the Islands Council, a badge was included, and is the first-ever instance of such a grant to a Scottish local authority.

The dexter supporters mentioned above were agreed for Shetland and Western Isles, while Orkney preferred to retain the fifteenth-century udaller (landowner) from the county council arms.

The coronet devised for the Islands Councils has a design of dolphins in gold; the blazon is "a circlet richly chased from which are issuant four dolphins two and two respectant naiant embowed Or".

5.   Arms for the District Councils

The DISTRICT COUNCILS have an achievement consisting of shield, coronet and motto. Lyon decided that there were to be no supporters and no crests, and that mottoes were to be invariably placed under the shield. These rules have been strictly observed except in five special cases.

The four City District Councils (Aberdeen, Dundee, Edinburgh and Glasgow), have been allowed, after some representations and discussions, to take over the achievements of the former counties of cities and Royal burghs. Since, in these four cases, the Chairman of the District Council has, under Statute, the title of "Lord Provost", it was accepted that there was a present-day-case, to reinforce the strong historical one, for these four Districts to have more elaborate arms than the other Districts. So Dundee, Edinburgh and Glasgow keep their crests (but without helmets and mantlings), supporters and mottoes, and Aberdeen its supporters and motto. The Aberdeen and Edinburgh mottoes remain above the shield, and Dundee keeps its two mottoes, one above and one under the shield. In all cases, however, the District Council coronet has been included; Aberdeen objected most strongly to this decision and has stated that it intends to use its arms without this "modern" addition.

Later on, in the case of Perth & Kinross, Lord Lyon Monteith Grant received local representations for the inclusion in the District Council's arms of the eagle in the arms of the city and Royal burgh of Perth. He agreed that, since Perth had once been Scotland's capital and had ranked second in precedence among the Scottish burghs, the District Council's arms could be placed on an eagle bearer, just as those of the city had been; thus he continued the use of a unique feature in Scottish civic heraldry which probably goes back to the fourteenth century.[6]

The coronet devised for the District Councils has a design of thistle-heads in gold and is blazoned "a circlet richly chased from which are issuant eight thistle-heads Or".

6. Some Comments on the Heraldry

General

We have sixty coats-of-arms to consider. We must first note that twenty-two of them can be regarded as re-grants of the arms of former authorities: county council arms have been passed on in fifteen cases (Moray, Angus, Fife, West Lothian, Midlothian, East Lothian, Clackmannan, Stirling, Tweeddale, Roxburgh, Berwickshire, Renfrew, Wigtown, Stewartry, and Orkney) and burgh arms in seven (Lochaber, City of Aberdeen, City of Dundee, Dunfermline, City of Edinburgh, City of Glasgow, and Motherwell). Then there are twelve instances where the arms which have been granted resemble very closely those of former authorities: the arms of Caithness, Ross & Cromarty, Kincardine & Deeside, Perth & Kinross, Ettrick & Lauderdale, Argyll & Bute, and Shetland, are all based on county council arms, and those of Kirkcaldy, Dumbarton, Hamilton, East Kilbride, and Annandale & Eskdale, on burgh arms. There are also thirteen other examples where the main features of the arms granted hark back to county council or burgh arms viz. Inverness, Nairn, North East Fife, Falkirk, Bearsden & Milngavie, Strathkelvin, Cumbernauld & Kilsyth, Monklands, Lanark, Inverclyde, Cunninghame, Cumnock & Doon Valley, and Nithsdale.

Here it is of interest to note that in these cases the original blazons have generally been closely followed. There has been little or no attempt at modernisation even in blazons as old as Aberdeen (1674), Perth & Kinross (1800), Kirkcaldy (c.1673), Edinburgh (1732), Roxburgh (1798), Dumbarton (c.1673), and Glasgow (1866). And so some inconsistencies were inevitable: for example, the Royal Tressure, which appears four times, is blazoned in three versions: in City of Aberdeen and Perth & Kinross, it is described as "a double tressure flowered and counter-flowered"; in Moray, it is "a double tressure flory counterflory", and in Ettrick & Lauderdale, simply "the Royal Tressure". Then the Roxburgh unicorn's tufted tail gets a special mention whereas nothing is said about the tails of the unicorns which support the coats of arms of the Regional and Islands Councils. But even in the modern blazons there are some stylistic variations, e.g. we have a plain English hedgehog in Eastwood but in Nithsdale it is called a hurcheon (following Nisbet's blazon for Maxwell, Earl of Nithsdale).[7] Or we see that twenty-four District Councils have their mottoes "under the Shield", nine "under the same", two "below the Shield", and two "below the same". Small eccentricities of this kind are the spice of heraldry and add to the interest of the subject.

The Shields

Remembering that seven out of the eight Regional coats of arms are of a pattern, i.e. each has an undivided shield bearing two ordinaries (a bordure and a saltire) and one sub-ordinary (an inescutcheon), we find that the sixty shields can be classified as shown below:

UNDIVIDED SHIELDS (42)

	Number	*Remarks*
Without Ordinaries or Sub-Ordinaries	15	One with bar; one with 3 bars; one with a fimbriated wavy closet; in base a mount appears twice, a rock twice, wavy (with 3 pallets) once, invected barry once.
With Ordinaries and Sub-Ordinaries		
Bordure, Saltire and Inescutcheon	7	One with cross on inescutcheon; all inescutcheons are fimbriated.
Chief, Bordure and Inescutcheon (2)	1	Chief wavy and per pale.
Saltire and Roundel	1	The roundel is *argent* i.e. a plate, is fimbriated and bears two wavy barrulets.

With Ordinaries

Bordure	1	
Chief	4	One wavy; one wavy per pale with a wavy bar below.
Chief, Cross and Saltire	1	Chief wavy with pale; mount in base.
Chief and Saltire	2	One chief with pale; one chief with bar wavy and two barrulets wavy.
Fess	3	One embattled and enarched; one wavy with two barrulets wavy.
Saltire	2	One with the sea in base.

With Sub-Ordinaries

Inescutcheon	3	Two with a mount in base.
Roundel	1	Base wavy; the roundel is *azure* i.e. a hurt.
Shakefork	1	
	42	

DIVIDED SHIELDS (18)

	Number	*Remarks*
Quarterly	5	–
Per Fess	7	One enhanced; one with per pale in chief; two wavy with per pale in chief; one with per pale in base and a chief per pale.
Per Pale	5	One with chief; one with chief enarched and per pale, one indented with chief.
Tierced in Pairle Reversed	1	–
	18	

Note: The blazons of these divided Shields can, of course, be further broken down.

The tinctures used are confined to the metals (or and argent), the commonest colours (gules, azure, sable and vert) and one fur (ermine), which appears three times. There are ten instances of a fimbriation (nine in gold, one in silver), two cases where the smallest diminutive of the pale, an endorse (one in gold, one in silver), is used to separate two divisions of identical colour, and one, where a fillet (in ermine) is used for the same purpose.

The lion is the commonest charge and there are many ships and allusions to the sea and to rivers. Clan and family associations figure prominently and there are several references to the ancient Scottish Earldoms and to patron saints, notably of burghs. Industry is well to the fore being represented by fishing, shipping, ship-building, agriculture, forestry, iron-smelting and steel-making, coal-mining, woollen manufacture and spinning. History and tradition have their place and are represented by charges recalling events like the saving of the Scottish Regalia in 1651/52 (Kincardine & Deeside), the Battle of Bannockburn (1314) (Stirling), the Norwegian connection (Orkney, Shetland), and high dignities like the Lordship of the Isles (Argyll & Bute, Western Isles) and the High Stewardship of Scotland (Renfrew, Kyle & Carrick). Well-known local landmarks appear:— Loch Leven Castle (Perth & Kinross), Malcolm's Tower (Dunfermline), Edinburgh Castle (City of Edinburgh), Antonine's Wall (Falkirk, Clydebank, Strathkelvin), Ettrick Forest (Ettrick & Lauderdale), Bothwell Brig (Hamilton), and the ancient East Wood (Eastwood). There is also an interesting modern reference to the well-known osprey colony at Loch Garten (Badenoch & Strathspey).

Mottoes, Crests and Supporters

Forty-three of the Authorities (one Regional, three Islands, and thirty-nine Districts) have *mottoes*, and one of the Districts, City of Dundee, has two. Except for three City Districts, Aberdeen, Dundee (one motto) and Edinburgh, all the mottoes are placed under the shield. Eighteen are in Latin, ten in English, nine in Scots, five in Gaelic, one in French and one in Old Norse. Fifteen of these mottoes have passed on from county councils and a like number from burghs.

There are only three examples of *crests*, all in the City Districts and, therefore, inherited from the Royal burghs. They are City of Dundee (a lily), City of Edinburgh (an anchor), and City of Glasgow (St Kentigern (without a halo)).

As mentioned above, *supporters* have only been allowed in the case of the eight Regional Councils which have registered arms, the three Islands Councils, the four City Districts, and Perth & Kinross (which has an eagle as bearer).

Coronets

The system of special coronets devised for the Regional Councils, the Islands Councils, and the District Councils has already been described.

7.   Arms for the Community Councils

The COMMUNITY COUNCILS, which could eventually number some thirteen hundred, may apply for and be granted armorial bearings. But since so far only ten Community Councils have done so, it is not proposed to make more than passing reference to them in this book. In any case it seems unlikely that many more will seek to record arms in the near future, if only because of the cost involved — now £173.

The ten Councils which have registered arms are Biggar, Duns, North Berwick, Hawick, Royal Burgh of Lanark, Royal Burgh of St Andrews, Bishopbriggs, Kelso,

Bathgate, and Royal Burgh of Jedburgh. As they all have a close connection with burghs of the same names, the burgh arms have been re-granted in each case, subject to the replacement of the burghal coronet by a Community Council one. In the case of Royal Burgh of Lanark, a burghal coronet has, by local request, been added to the ancient burgh arms. Details are given in Appendix III.

The coronet devised for the Community Councils has a design of thistle leaves and pine cones in gold and is blazoned "a circlet richly chased from which are issuant four thistle leaves and four pine cones Or".

PART II

The Arms of the Councils

INTRODUCTORY

In this, the main part of the book, I have dealt in detail with the coats of arms of the individual Regional, District and Islands Councils. As mentioned on page 8 above, eight of the nine Regional Councils, forty-nine of the fifty-three District Councils, and all three Islands Councils, have recorded arms; these are all described and illustrated. The dates of the Lyon Register Entries are of no particular significance, since, in all of these cases, the Letters Patent state that the arms are to be borne by each Council with effect from 16 May 1975.

For sake of completeness, I have also included brief details of the non-heraldic symbols used by the non-armigerous Councils.

Since there could be as many as thirteen hundred Community Councils and only ten have so far registered arms, I have merely stated the current position in Appendix III; as I have already indicated, it seems unlikely that many of them will apply for grants of arms.

The various individual articles are arranged in chapters under Regions, starting with Highland Region, as in Part III of Schedule 1 to the Local Government (Scotland) Act 1973. The Regional Council comes first and then the District Councils in the order given in the Schedule. The Islands Councils have a chapter on their own at the end.

Each article is prefaced by a short note describing the area administered by the Council; these are the same as those given in Schedule 1 to the Act, except where significant changes have since been approved by the Boundaries Commission. Since the passing of the Act the Secretary of State for Scotland has approved three changes of name: Bishopbriggs & Kirkintilloch has become Strathkelvin, Cumbernauld is now Cumbernauld & Kilsyth, and Merrick has changed to Wigtown.

It should always be understood that, where a re-grant or take-over of the arms of a former authority was permitted, this was invariably subject to the addition of the appropriate coronet or to its substitution for the existing burghal or county one. I have, however mentioned the coronets in the City Districts where special circumstances apply. Then, in referring to the arms of former authorities, I have confined the use of the word "matriculated" to burghs whose arms were recorded before 1940.

There are several references to Scottish Kings. Apart from William the Lion, all the Kings are called by their official numbers. Thus Malcolm Canmore is King Malcolm III, and Robert the Bruce, King Robert I. Queen Mary is referred to by her customary style of Mary, Queen of Scots.

The drawings have been specially prepared for the book by Miss Jennifer Mitchell, the Herald Painter to the Lyon Court. They are intended to stand as an effective set and we have endeavoured to make them as consistent as possible. The hatchings used to depict the various metals, colours and fur are shown in the diagram below; these hatchings have been used wherever the scale of drawing has permitted.

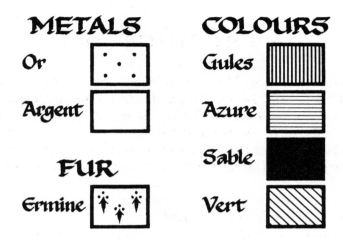

HIGHLAND REGION

The HIGHLAND Region consists of (1) the county of Caithness, (2) the county of Nairn, (3) the county of Sutherland, (4) the county of Inverness (except the districts of Barra, Harris, North Uist and South Uist), (5) The county of Ross & Cromarty (except the burgh of Stornoway and the district of Lewis), (6) the burgh of Grantown-on-Spey and the district of Cromdale, in the county of Moray, and (7) in the county of Argyll, the district of Ardnamurchan and the electoral divisions of Ballachulish and Kinlochleven, from the district of North Lorn. The Region is divided into eight Districts: Caithness, Sutherland, Ross & Cromarty, Skye & Lochalsh, Lochaber, Inverness, Badenoch & Strathspey, and Nairn.

HIGHLAND REGIONAL COUNCIL

Azure, a saltire Argent, surmounted at the fess point by an inescutcheon Gules, fimbriated Or, and charged with a star Argent, a bordure counter-compony of the First and Second.

Above the Shield is placed a coronet appropriate to a statutory Region, *videlicet*:– a circlet richly chased, from which are issuant four thistles leaved (one and two halves visible) Or; and on a Compartment below the Shield are set for *Supporters*, dexter, a stag Or, and sinister, a unicorn Argent, armed, maned and unguled Or, and gorged with a collar Gules, from which is pendant an oval badge Azure, fimbriated Or, charged with a saltire Argent.

(Lyon Register lix, 27:25 July 1975)

HIGHLAND REGIONAL COUNCIL has its headquarters at Inverness.

The Council's arms follow the basic Regional design of a St Andrew's cross within a blue and silver bordure and surmounted by a red inescutcheon with a gold fimbriation. The inescutcheon is charged with a silver star as this is a feature which appears in the arms of some of the best known Highland families like Sutherland, Brodie and Macrae, and also on the banner of the ancient province of Moray, which included much of the southern part of the Region. The dexter supporter is a Highland stag, and the sinister supporter the unicorn common to all the Regional Councils' coats of arms.

CAITHNESS DISTRICT COUNCIL

Azure, a galley Or, the sail thereof Argent charged with a raven Sable, and in chief two crosier heads of the Second.

Above the Shield is placed a coronet appropriate to a statutory District, *videlicet*:– a circlet richly chased, from which are issuant eight thistle-heads (three and two halves visible) Or; and in an Escrol under the Shield this *Motto* "Wark to God".

(Lyon Register lix, 64: 1 November 1977)

CAITHNESS DISTRICT COUNCIL administers an area comprising the county of Caithness.[1] Its headquarters are at Wick.

The arms recall those granted to Caithness County Council in 1935. The gold galley on the blue field alludes to the ancient Earldom of Caithness and on its sail is the black raven of the Norse Jarls whose lands included not only Orkney and Shetland but also Caithness and Sutherland. The crosier heads in chief refer to St Fergus (patron saint of the Royal burgh of Wick) and to St Peter (patron saint of the burgh of Thurso) and thus to the two burghs of the District.

SUTHERLAND DISTRICT COUNCIL administers an area comprising the county of Sutherland and the electoral division of Kincardine from the district of Tain in the county of Ross & Cromarty.[1] The Council's headquarters are at Golspie.

The Council has not registered arms and uses a plain seal bearing the legend "The District Council of Sutherland".

ROSS & CROMARTY DISTRICT COUNCIL

Per fess Gules and Azure: in chief three lions rampant Argent, in base an endorse of the Last between dexter, a stag's head cabossed, and sinister, a sun in its splendour between five mullets Or.

Above the Shield is placed a coronet appropriate to a statutory District, *videlicet:*– a circlet richly chased, from which are issuant eight thistle-heads (three and two halves visible) Or; and in an Escrol under the Shield this *Motto* "Dread God and Do Well".

(Lyon Register lix, 26: 27 November 1975)

ROSS & CROMARTY DISTRICT COUNCIL administers an area comprising the following parts of the county of Ross & Cromarty: the burghs of Cromarty, Dingwall, Fortrose, Invergordon, and Tain, the districts of Avoch, Dingwall, Fearn, Fortrose, Gairloch, Invergordon, Lochbroom, Lochcarron, Muir of Ord, and, from the district of Tain, the electoral division of Edderton & Tain. The Council's headquarters are at Dingwall.

The arms, which are based on those granted to Ross & Cromarty County Council in 1957, refer to the four main families of the District and to its headquarters town. The silver lions on their red field are for Ross and the ancient Earldom; the gold caberfeidh on blue is for Mackenzie; the sun and the firmament come from the arms of the Royal burgh of Dingwall (matriculated 1897) – this old device appears on a 1438–39 impression of the burgh seal and the matrix is regarded as of thirteenth century manufacture.[2] The Motto effectively combines the Munro "Dread God" with the last part of the Urquhart "Mean Weil, Speak Weil and Doe Weil".

SKYE & LOCHALSH DISTRICT COUNCIL administers an area comprising the district of Skye in the county of Inverness and the South West district in the county of Ross & Cromarty. Its headquarters are at Portree.

The Council has not registered arms. It uses a plain seal bearing its name in "Celtic" lettering; the type used is called American Uncial.

LOCHABER DISTRICT COUNCIL

Argent, two Lochaber axes, heads upwards and blades outwards, saltirewise, intertwined with a chaplet of oak; in chief an imperial crown, all Proper.

Above the Shield is placed a coronet appropriate to a statutory District, *videlicet:*– a circlet richly chased, from which are issuant eight thistle-heads (three and two halves visible) Or; and in an Escrol under the Shield this *Motto* "A D'h Aindeoin Co Theireadh E".

(Lyon Register lix, 14: 24 August 1976)

LOCHABER DISTRICT COUNCIL administers an area comprising (1) the district of Ardnamurchan and the electoral divisions of Ballachulish and Kinlochleven, from the district of North Lorn, in the county of Argyll, and (2) the burgh of Fort William and the district of Lochaber, in the county of Inverness. The Council has its headquarters at Fort William.

The Council has been allowed to take over the arms matriculated by the burgh of Fort William in 1930. The crossed Lochaber axes are symbolic of the District whose name they bear and also recall the Battle of Inverlochy fought in 1645 between the Marquess of Montrose and the Campbells. The oak branches are the plant badge of Clan Cameron, the main family of the area, while the crown recalls the two Royal names (Maryburgh and Fort William) which the headquarters town has borne. The whole device is said to have been based on the badge of the Lochaber Fencibles (embodied 1798, disbanded 1802). The Gaelic Motto means "Gainsay it who dare" and is the same as that of Macdonald of Clanranald; it is said to have been associated with the Lochaber Fencibles because one of their captains was a Ronald Macdonald.[3]

INVERNESS DISTRICT COUNCIL

Per fess enhanced Azure and Gules, a barrulet wavy enhanced Argent; in base Our Lord upon the Cross Proper between a crescent and a mullet Or, and in chief between dexter, a cornucopia, and sinister, a fraise Argent, on a pale Or a cat saliant Proper.

Above the Shield is placed a coronet appropriate to a statutory District, *videlicet*:– a circlet richly chased, from which are issuant eight thistle-heads (three and two halves visible) Or; and in an Escrol under the Shield this *Motto* "Concordia et Fidelitas".

(Lyon Register lix, 34: 7 September 1975)

INVERNESS DISTRICT COUNCIL administers an area in the county of Inverness comprising the burgh of Inverness and the districts of Aird and Inverness. Its headquarters are at Inverness.

The main features of the arms reflect those of the Royal burgh of Inverness (matriculated 1900) viz., "Gules, Our Lord upon the Cross Proper". These come from the obverse of the oldest known burgh seal of which an impression dated 1439 is on record;[4] the representation of Our Lord on the Cross probably refers to the important side altar of the Holy Cross in the pre-Reformation parish church which was dedicated to the Virgin Mary. The gold crescent and star (the moon and the sun) have been added in accordance with old heraldic practice followed in coats of arms bearing representations of Christ and of saints. The cornucopia in the chief was the burgh crest, probably referring to its trade and prosperity, and it is accompanied by a Mackintosh cat for the Inverness district and by a Fraser fraise (or cinquefoil) for the Aird district. The wavy barrulet alludes to the rivers Beauly and Ness. The burgh's Latin Motto – "Concord and Fidelity" – has been retained.

BADENOCH & STRATHSPEY DISTRICT COUNCIL

Or, an osprey volant grasping a fish in its talons Proper, a chief wavy per pale, dexter, Azure a boar's head couped Or and sinister, Gules an antique crown also Or, a bar wavy enhanced per fess wavy Argent and Azure.

Above the Shield is placed a coronet appropriate to a statutory District, *videlicet:*– a circlet richly chased, from which are issuant eight thistle-heads (three and two halves visible) Or; and in an Escrol below the same this Motto "Tre Oideas Agus Creideamh".

(Lyon Register lix, 65: 18 January 1979)

BADENOCH & STRATHSPEY DISTRICT COUNCIL administers an area comprising the burgh of Kingussie and the district of Badenoch, in the county of Inverness, and the burgh of Grantown-on-Spey and the district of Cromdale, in the county of Moray. Its headquarters are at Kingussie.

The arms show in chief (1) a Gordon boar's head on its blue field, for Badenoch and Kingussie: the Lordship of Badenoch has, since the fifteenth century, been held by the Gordon family now represented by the Marquess of Huntly, and Kingussie was made a burgh of barony in favour of Alexander, 1st Earl of Huntly in 1464;[5] (2) a Grant crown on its red field, for Strathspey and Grantown-on-Spey; the Grants have been the historic family of Strathspey since the fifteenth century. The wavy division of the shield and the bar wavy are for the river Spey. In base there is a more modern reference, to the well-known colony of ospreys established since 1959 at Loch Garten in the centre of the District. The Gaelic Motto means "By Tradition and Faith" and was a local suggestion.

NAIRN DISTRICT COUNCIL

Azure, a figure of Saint Ninian holding in his dexter hand an open book, his crosier in his sinister hand and pendant from the wrist thereof a manacle all Proper, between dexter, a sun radiant Or and sinister, a mullet Argent; on a chief Or, two water budgets Sable.

Above the Shield is placed a coronet appropriate to a statutory District, *videlicet*:– a circlet richly chased, from which are issuant eight thistle-heads (three and two halves visible) Or; and in an Escrol under the same this *Motto* "Unite and Be Mindful".

(Lyon Register lix, 59: 10 August 1976)

NAIRN DISTRICT COUNCIL administers an area comprising the county of Nairn. Its headquarters are at Nairn.

The arms show St Ninian, patron saint of the Royal burgh of Nairn and the main feature of its arms (matriculated 1939). The saint appears on the oldest known burgh seal of which a 1479 impression is on record.[6] The influence of Fearn Abbey, on the opposite side of the Moray Firth, whose first Abbot came from Whithorn and which possessed some of St Ninian's relics, led to his adoption as Nairn's patron saint. The blue field is for the sea while the sun and the star have been included in accordance with old heraldic practice in coats of arms depicting saints. The sun has been made radiant to recall the burgh's Motto "Sole Valemus" and its excellent sunshine record. The star and the water budgets appeared in the arms granted to the County Council in 1927 and respectively refer to the Nairnshire families of Baillie of Lochloy and Rose of Kilravock. The Motto, which comes from the same source, combines the mottoes of two other local families, Brodie of Brodie and Campbell of Cawdor.

3

GRAMPIAN REGION

The GRAMPIAN Region consists of the county of the city of Aberdeen, the county of Aberdeen, the county of Kincardine, the county of Banff, and the county of Moray (except the burgh of Grantown-on-Spey and the district of Cromdale). The Region is divided into five Districts: Moray, Banff & Buchan, Gordon, City of Aberdeen, and Kincardine & Deeside.

GRAMPIAN REGIONAL COUNCIL

Azure, a saltire Argent, surmounted at the fess point by an inescutcheon Gules, fimbriated Or, and charged with a cross-crosslet fitchée Or, a bordure counter-compony of the First and Second.

Above the Shield is placed a coronet appropriate to a statutory Region, *videlicet*:– a circlet richly chased, from which are issuant four thistles leaved (one and two halves visible) Or; and on a Compartment below the Shield are set for *Supporters,* dexter, a ptarmigan Proper, and sinister, a unicorn Argent, armed, maned and unguled Or, and gorged with a collar Gules, from which is pendant an oval badge Azure, fimbriated Or, charged with a saltire Argent.

(Lyon Register, lix, 13:3 March 1975)

GRAMPIAN REGIONAL COUNCIL has its headquarters at Aberdeen.

The Council's arms follow the basic Regional design of a St Andrew's cross within a blue and silver bordure and surmounted by an inescutcheon with a gold fimbriation. The inescutcheon is charged with a gold cross-crosslet, a feature taken from the arms of the ancient Earldom of Mar. The dexter supporter is a ptarmigan, a typical bird of the Region, and the sinister supporter is the unicorn common to all the Regional Councils' coats of arms.

MORAY DISTRICT COUNCIL

Quarterly: 1st and 4th, Azure, three mullets Argent; 2nd and 3rd, Argent, three cushions within a double tressure flory counterflory Gules.

Above the Shield is placed a coronet appropriate to a statutory District, *videlicet*:– a circlet richly chased, from which are issuant eight thistle-heads (three and two halves visible) Or; and in an Escrol below the same this *Motto* "Sub Spe".

(Lyon Register lix, 61:22 July 1977)

MORAY DISTRICT COUNCIL administers an area comprising (1) the county of Moray (except the burgh of Grantown-on-Spey and the district of Cromdale), and (2) in the county of Banff, the burghs of Aberlour, Buckie, Cullen, Dufftown, Findochty, Keith, and Portknockie, along with the districts of Buckie, Cullen (except the electoral division of Fordyce), Dufftown, and Keith. The Council's headquarters are at Elgin.

The Council has been allowed to take over the arms granted to Moray County Council in 1927. They show three silver stars on a blue field from the banner of the ancient Province of Moray, along with three red cushions within the Royal tressure on a silver field, as these were the original arms of Thomas Randolph, the famous Lieutenant of King Robert I, who was created Earl of Moray in 1312. The Latin Motto – "In hope" – is that of the family of Dunbar, which has long associations with the District; it also provides a pleasing punning reference to the river Spey which flows through much of the area.

BANFF & BUCHAN DISTRICT COUNCIL

Argent, a lion passant guardant Gules, crowned with an antique crown Or; on a chief wavy Azure three fish fretted Proper between two garbs of the Third banded Vert.

Above the Shield is placed a coronet appropriate to a statutory District, *videlicet*:– a circlet richly chased, from which are issuant eight thistle-heads (three and two halves visible) Or.

(Lyon Register lix, 37: 1 October 1975)

BANFF & BUCHAN DISTRICT COUNCIL administers an area comprising (1) the burghs of Aberchirder, Banff, Macduff, and Portsoy, the districts of Aberchirder and Banff, and from the district of Cullen, the electoral division of Fordyce, all in the county of Banff, and (2) in the county of Aberdeen, the burghs of Fraserburgh, Peterhead, Rosehearty, and Turriff, the districts of Deer and Turriff, and the electoral division of Cruden from the district of Ellon. The Council's headquarters are at Banff.

    The arms show (for Banff) the Ogilvy lion with a Grant antique crown which appeared in the arms granted to Banff County Council in 1953; this recalls the Earldom of Seafield and two of the principal families of the area. In the chief (for Buchan) the blue and wavy denote the sea, the garbs come from the arms of the ancient Earldom of Buchan, and the fish stand for the fishing industry of which Fraserburgh and Peterhead are the main centres.

GORDON DISTRICT COUNCIL administers an area in the county of Aberdeen comprising the burghs of Ellon, Huntly, Inverurie, Kintore, and Old Meldrum, the districts of Aberdeen (except the electoral divisions of Bucksburn, Newhills Landward, Old Machar, and Stoneywood, and the parishes of Drumoak, Dyce and Peterculter), Alford, Ellon, (except the electoral division of Cruden), Garioch, and Huntly. The Council's headquarters are at Inverurie.

    The Council has not registered arms. It uses as an emblem (which also appears on its seal) a hexagonal device in the centre of which the capital letters "GD" appear in outline type on a black background.

CITY OF ABERDEEN DISTRICT COUNCIL

Gules, three towers triple-towered within a double tressure flowered and counterflowered Argent;

Supported by two leopards Proper.

Above the Shield is placed a coronet appropriate to a statutory District, *videlicet:*– a circlet richly chased, from which are issuant eight thistle-heads (three and two halves visible) Or; and in an Escrol over the same this *Motto* "Bon Accord".

(Lyon Register lix, 7: 4 November 1976)

CITY OF ABERDEEN DISTRICT COUNCIL administers an area comprising (1) the county of the city of Aberdeen, (2) the electoral divisions of Bucksburn, Newhills Landward, Old Machar, and Stoneywood, and the parishes of Dyce and Peterculter, from the district of Aberdeen in the county of Aberdeen, and (3) the electoral division of Nigg, from the district of Lower Deeside in the county of Kincardine. The Council's headquarters are at Aberdeen.

The Council has been re-granted the arms matriculated by the city and Royal burgh of Aberdeen in 1674, subject to the addition of the District Council coronet. These are a development of early (but not the oldest) seals of the city of which impressions dated 1430 and 1440 are on record.[1] The three triple towers are said to refer to the three fortified hills, Castle, Port and St Catherine's, on which the city had its origins. The Royal tressure is traditionally regarded as having been granted in 1308 by King Robert I in recognition of the outstanding services given by the burghers in capturing Aberdeen Castle and expelling the English from the city; but there appears to be good historical evidence to support the view that it only dates from the reign of King James I (1406–1437) and may have been granted by him, along with the supporters (originally more like lions and similar to those used by King James himself) because Aberdeen was one of the burghs which agreed to underwrite his expenses during his exile in England.[2] The Motto, however, may well have originated during the 1308 siege: the Patent of Arms granted to the city in 1674 states that "the word 'Bon Accord' was given them (the citizens) by King Robert the Bruce for killing all the English in one night in their town, their word being that night 'Bon Accord'".[3]

KINCARDINE & DEESIDE DISTRICT COUNCIL

Gules, the Sword of State and the Sceptre of Scotland in saltire, in chief the Crown of Scotland Or, a closet wavy reduced Azure fimbriated Argent; on a base wavy Vert, three pallets Or.

Above the Shield is placed a coronet appropriate to a statutory District, *videlicet*:– a circlet richly chased, from which are issuant eight thistle-heads (three and two halves visible) Or; and in an Escrol below the Shield this Motto "Laus Deo".

(Lyon Register lix, 63: 27 September 1977)

KINCARDINE & DEESIDE DISTRICT COUNCIL administers an area comprising (1) the burgh of Ballater, the district of Deeside, and the parish of Drumoak from the district of Aberdeen, in the county of Aberdeen, and (2) the following parts of the county of Kincardine: the burghs of Banchory, Inverbervie, Laurencekirk, and Stonehaven, the districts of Laurencekirk, St Cyrus, Stonehaven, and Upper Deeside, and, from the district of Lower Deeside, the electoral divisions of Banchory-Devenick and Maryculter. The Council's headquarters are at Stonehaven.

The arms are based on those granted in 1927 to Kincardine County Council. They recall the preservation of the Scottish Regalia after the coronation of King Charles II at Scone in 1651. Sent for safety to the Earl Marischal's stronghold of Dunnottar Castle, near Stonehaven, they were saved from the besieging Cromwellian troops by the initiative of George Ogilvy of Barras, Governor of the Castle, and Mr James Grainger, Minister of the adjacent parish of Kinneff.[4] The crown, sword, and sceptre were smuggled out of the castle and buried under the floor of Kinneff church, where they remained until the Restoration in 1660. The Honours of Scotland thus occupy the centre of the shield, the red and gold colours being those of the Scottish Royal House; they can also recall the close modern connection of Deeside with the Royal Family. The lower part of the shield represents Deeside, the wavy closet (a demi-bar) being for the river and the gold and green for the surrounding country. The Latin Motto – "Praise to God" – is that of the Viscount of Arbuthnott; it was chosen in 1927 because the 14th Viscount was then Lord Lieutenant of the county of Kincardine.

4

TAYSIDE REGION

The TAYSIDE Region consists of the county of the city of Dundee, the county of Angus, the county of Kinross, and the county of Perth (except the burghs of Callander, Doune, and Dunblane, the Western district (apart from the electoral division of Ardoch), and, in the Central district, the parish of Muckhart). The Region is divided into three Districts: Angus, City of Dundee, and Perth & Kinross.

TAYSIDE REGIONAL COUNCIL

Azure, a saltire Argent, surmounted at the fess point by an inescutcheon Gules, fimbriated Or, and charged with a fleur-de-lis Argent and in chief a bar wavy of the Last, a bordure counter-compony of the First and Second.

Above the Shield is placed a coronet appropriate to a statutory Region, *videlicet*:– a circlet richly chased, from which are issuant four thistles leaved (one and two halves visible) Or; and on a Compartment below the Shield are set for *Supporters*, dexter, an Angus bull Proper, and sinister, a unicorn Argent, armed, maned and unguled Or, and gorged with a collar Gules, from which is pendant an oval badge Azure, fimbriated Or, charged with a saltire Argent.

(Lyon Register lix, 17: 21 May 1975)

TAYSIDE REGIONAL COUNCIL has its headquarters at Dundee.
The Council's arms follow the basic Regional design of a St Andrew's cross within

a blue and silver bordure and surmounted by a red inescutcheon with a gold fimbriation. The inescutcheon is charged with a silver bar wavy to denote the river Tay, from which the Region gets its name, and a silver fleur-de-lis in reference to the city of Dundee and its patron saint, the Virgin Mary. The dexter supporter is one of the famous Angus bulls, and the sinister supporter is the unicorn common to all the Regional Councils' coats of arms. The Council specially asked for a representation of water to be included in the compartment.

ANGUS DISTRICT COUNCIL

Quarterly: 1st, Argent, a lion passant guardant Gules, imperially crowned Or; 2nd, Gules, a cinquefoil Or; 3rd, Or, a fess chequy Azure and Argent, surmounted of a bend Gules charged with three buckles of the field; 4th, Argent, a man's heart Gules, imperially crowned Or, on a chief Azure three mullets of the field.

Above the Shield is placed a coronet appropriate to a statutory District, *videlicet*:— a circlet richly chased, from which are issuant eight thistle-heads (three and two halves visible) Or; and in an Escrol under the Shield this *Motto* "Lippen on Angus".

(Lyon Register lix, 41:27 November 1975)

ANGUS DISTRICT COUNCIL administers an area in the county of Angus comprising the burghs of Arbroath, Brechin, Carnoustie, Forfar, Kirriemuir, and Montrose, the districts of Brechin, Carnoustie, Forfar, Kirriemuir, and Montrose, and the parish of Newtyle from the district of Monifieth. The Council's headquarters are at Forfar.

The Council has been re-granted the arms granted to the County Council in 1927. These recall the four families which have held the Earldom of Angus viz., Gillibride (from c.1150), d'Umfraville (from c.1240), Stewart of Bonkyll (from 1329), and Douglas (from 1389). The coats of arms chosen to represent the first two of these families are those associated with their Earldoms by Lord Lyon Balfour Paul in his work *The Scots Peerage* (1904–1914) and not their own family coats.[1] The Scots Motto means "Trust in Angus".

CITY OF DUNDEE DISTRICT COUNCIL administers an area comprising the county of the city of Dundee, the burgh of Monifieth and the district of Monifieth (except the electoral division of Newtyle & Kettins), in the County of Angus, and, in the county of Perth, the electoral division of Longforgan from the district of Perth. The Council has its headquarters at Dundee.

CITY OF DUNDEE DISTRICT COUNCIL

Azure, a pot of three growing lilies Argent.

Above the Shield is placed a coronet appropriate to a statutory District, *videlicet*:– a circlet richly chased, from which are issuant eight thistle-heads (three and two halves visible) Or; and on a Wreath of the Colours is set for *Crest* a lily Argent; and in an Escrol over the same this *Motto* "Dei Donum", and in another Escrol under the Shield this *Motto* "Prudentia et Candore", the said Shield having for *Supporters* two dragons, wings elevated, their tails nowed together underneath, Vert.

(Lyon Register lix, 5: 2 October 1975)

The Council has been re-granted the arms of the city and Royal burgh of Dundee (matriculated 1673 and (revised) 1932) subject to the omission of the helmet and mantling and to a change of coronet. These follow very closely the heraldic device on an old seal of the city of which an impression dated 1416 is on record.[2] The lilies and the blue field are for the Virgin Mary, to whom the parish church of Dundee is dedicated; the white lily is one of the flowers specially associated with her. It has been suggested that the dragon supporters symbolised the sea and the city's overseas trade but they may well be derived from the lions' heads and legs of the faldstool on which the figure of St Clement sits on the obverse of the fifteenth century burgh seal.[3] The first Latin Motto is said to be connected with a legend which tells how David, Earl of Huntingdon and brother of King William the Lion, landed here after a storm on his return from the Crusades about 1190 and called the place "Donum Dei" – "God's Gift"; this, however has nothing whatever to do with the name Dundee which almost certainly comes from the Gaelic and means "fort on the Tay". The second Latin Motto – "With Thought and Purity" – was a later addition and is probably a further reference to the city's patron saint, the Virgin Mary.

PERTH & KINROSS DISTRICT COUNCIL

Or, a lion rampant Gules, armed and langued Azure, standing on a compartment or mount Proper and brandishing in his dexter paw a scimitar of the Last, all within a double tressure flowered and counterflowered of the Second; on an inescutcheon Argent, on an island Proper in a loch undy Azure and of the field, a castle also Proper; the Shield being surmounted on the breast of an eagle with two necks displayed Sable, gorged with a coronet appropriate to a statutory District, *videlicet*:– a circlet richly chased, from which are issuant eight thistle-heads (three and two halves visible) Or; and in an Escrol under the Shield this *Motto* "Pro Lege et Libertate".

(Lyon Register lix, 60: 9 February 1977)

PERTH & KINROSS DISTRICT COUNCIL administers an area comprising (1) the county of Kinross, (2) the parish of Kettins from the district of Monifieth, in the county of Angus, and (3) the following parts of the county of Perth: the burghs of Aberfeldy, Abernethy, Alyth, Auchterarder, Blairgowrie & Rattray, Coupar Angus, Crieff, Perth, and Pitlochry, the districts of Central (except the parish of Muckhart), Eastern, Highland, and Perth (except the electoral district of Longforgan), and the electoral division of Ardoch in the Western district. The Council's headquarters are at Perth.

The arms combine the main features of the arms granted to the County of Perth in 1800 with those granted to Kinross County Council in 1927. They have been placed on an eagle bearer similar to that which appeared in the arms of the city and Royal burgh of Perth (matriculated c.1673). The Perthshire arms, which were designed and presented to the county by the 10th Earl of Kinnoull (Lord Lyon King of Arms 1796–1804), were originally closely connected with the Local Militia and Volunteer Forces, and were inherited by the County Council in 1890. They show a red lion standing on a mount and brandishing a scimitar – obviously a Scottish lion ready to defend his country; such a device appeared on a Perthshire Militia Troop colour dated 1684, an example of which is preserved in Blair Castle.[4] The addition of the Royal treasure recalls the many connections of the Royal House with Perthshire and can also allude to the fact that it appears in the arms of several of the most notable Perthshire families e.g. Hay, Drummond, Stewart and Murray, as represented by the Earls of Kinnoull, Perth, Moray and Mansfield, and, in the case of the last two, also by the Dukes of Atholl; it also appeared in the arms of the city and Royal burgh of Perth. The mount on which the lion stands could refer to the Drummond Earls of Perth, whose arms stand on a compartment described by Nisbet as "like to a green hill semée of caltraps".[5] The arms of Kinross County Council are on the inescutcheon. They show a representation of Loch Leven Castle, which stands on an island in the loch of the same name beside Kinross burgh; this is the castle where Mary, Queen of Scots, was imprisoned and forced to abdicate in favour of her son King James VI in 1567, and from which she made her famous escape in the following year. The Latin Motto – "For Law and Liberty" – was that used by the County of Perth and by Perth County Council.

The eagle bearer was allowed as a special case to mark the fact that the city of Perth was a former capital of Scotland and took precedence over all the Scottish burghs, except Edinburgh.

5

FIFE REGION

The FIFE Region consists of the county of Fife. It is divided into three Districts: Kirkcaldy, North East Fife, and Dunfermline.

FIFE REGIONAL COUNCIL

Argent, a knight armed at all points on a horse at full speed, in his dexter hand a sword erect, all Proper, his surcoat Argent, on his sinister arm a shield Or, charged with a lion rampant Gules, the visor of his helmet shut, over which on a wreath of his liveries with a mantling of the Fourth doubled of the Third, is set a lion rampant, issuing out of the wreath, of the Fourth, the caparisons of the horse of the Last, fimbriated of the Third, and thereon six shields of the Last, each charged with a lion rampant of the Fourth.

Above the Shield is placed a coronet appropriate to a statutory Region *videlicet*:– a circlet richly chased, from which are issuant four thistles leaved (one and two halves visible) Or; and on a Compartment below the Shield, on which in an Escrol is set this *Motto* "Virtute et Opera", are set for *Supporters*, dexter, the figure of Saint Servanus Proper vested Argent, and sinister, a unicorn Argent, armed, maned and unguled Or, and gorged with a collar Gules, from which is pendant an oval badge Azure, fimbriated Or, charged with a saltire Argent.

(Lyon Register lix, 53: 3 March 1976)

FIFE REGIONAL COUNCIL has its headquarters at Glenrothes.

The Council has been allowed to take over the arms granted to Fife County Council in 1927 because it is the only Regional Council whose area is co-terminous with that of a county; to these arms have been added supporters and a Regional Council coronet.

The arms are based on a seal of Duncan, Earl of Fife, of which an impression dated 1360 is on record and described as "an armed knight on horseback at full speed, a sword in his right hand, and on his left arm a shield charged with a lion rampant, which is repeated on the caparisons of the horse".[1] This representation of "The Thane of Fife" has long been regarded as the county emblem. It appeared on a colour of the Fife Fencible Cavalry (disbanded 1797) and was used in the nineteenth century by the County Yeomanry.[2] The Latin Motto – "By Virtue and Energy" was that of Duff of Braco and is now used by the Dukes of Fife. The dexter supporter, St Servanus, is the saint specially associated with the Fife burgh of Culross and its Abbey, while the sinister supporter is the unicorn common to all the Regional Councils' coats of arms.

KIRKCALDY DISTRICT COUNCIL

Azure, an abbey of three pyramids Argent, each charged with a cross pattée Or, between in chief dexter a garb and sinister a buckle and in base a lymphad, sails furled, oars in action, all of the Last.

Above the Shield is placed a coronet appropriate to a statutory District, *videlicet*:– a circlet richly chased, from which are issuant eight thistle-heads (three and two halves visible) Or; and in an Escrol under the Shield this *Motto* "Vigilando Munio".

(Lyon Register lix, 39: 17 October 1975)

KIRKCALDY DISTRICT COUNCIL administers an area in the county of Fife comprising the burghs of Buckhaven & Methil, Burntisland, Kinghorn, Kirkcaldy Leslie, Leven, and Markinch, the districts of Glenrothes, Kirkcaldy (except that part of the electoral division of Auchtertool within the Gray Park polling district), and Wemyss, and, from the district of Lochgelly, the electoral divisions of Auchterderran, Denend, Kinglassie and New Carden. The Council's headquarters are at Kirkcaldy.

The arms have as their main feature the arms matriculated by the Royal burgh of Kirkcaldy in c.1673. The abbey has three pyramids or towers each of which is ensigned (rather than charged) with a cross. It may refer to the church of Kirkcaldy dedicated in 1242 to St Bryce, a disciple of St Martin of Tours,[3] or it may have some connection with the west gable of Dunfermline Abbey,[4] since Kirkcaldy was a burgh of the Abbot of Dunfermline in the fourteenth and fifteenth centuries.[5] To the Kirkcaldy arms have been added a gold buckle to mark the Leslie connection with part of the District, a garb in reference to its agricultural interests, and a galley for the shipping, fishing and other sea-faring interests of its coastal towns. The Latin Motto – "I guard by watching" – was the motto of the Royal burgh of Kirkcaldy.

NORTH EAST FIFE DISTRICT COUNCIL

Quarterly: 1st, Gules, three crowns of myrtle Or; 2nd, Argent, on a mount in base the figure of Saint Andrew Proper bearing his cross in front of him Argent; 3rd, Argent, on a base undy Azure and of the Last a lymphad, sails furled, Sable, flagged Gules; 4th Gules, in chief a garb Or, banded Vert, and in base a plough also Or, share Argent.

Above the Shield is placed a coronet appropriate to a statutory District, *videlicet:*– a circlet richly chased, from which are issuant eight thistle-heads (three and two halves visible) Or; and in an Escrol under the Shield this *Motto* "Steadfast".

(Lyon Register lix, 58:10 February 1977)

NORTH EAST FIFE DISTRICT COUNCIL administers an area comprising the burghs of Auchtermuchty, Crail, Cupar, Elie & Earlsferry, Falkland, Kilrenny Anstruther Easter & Anstruther Wester, Ladybank, Newburgh, Newport-on-Tay, Pittenweem, St Andrews, St Monance, and Tayport, and the districts of Cupar and St Andrews, all in the county of Fife. The Council's headquarters are at Cupar.

The arms show (1) three crowns of myrtle on a red field, from the arms of the Royal burgh of Cupar (matriculated 1929) – such a device appears to have been used by the burgh at least from the middle of the seventeenth century;[6] (2) St Andrew with his cross, from the arms of the Royal burgh of St Andrews (matriculated 1912) – the saint appears on a burgh seal of which a 1357 impression is on record;[7] (3) a galley in the sea, in reference to the sea-faring and fishing interests of the coastal towns; (4) a garb and a plough for the landward parts and their dependence on agriculture – the red and gold colours of Fife are predominant. The Motto is conventional.

DUNFERMLINE DISTRICT COUNCIL

Azure, on a rock Proper two lions supporting a tower with four steps Argent, masoned Sable, windows and portcullis Gules.

Above the Shield is placed a coronet appropriate to a statutory District, *videlicet*:– a circlet richly chased, from which are issuant eight thistle-heads (three and two halves visible) Or; and in an Escrol under the Shield this *Motto* "Esto Rupes Inaccessa".

(Lyon Register lix, 43: 16 February 1976)

DUNFERMLINE DISTRICT COUNCIL administers an area comprising the following parts of the county of Fife: the burghs of Cowdenbeath, Culross, Dunfermline, Inverkeithing, and Lochgelly, the districts of Dunfermline, Lochgelly (except for the electoral divisions of Auchterderran, Denend, Kinglassie, and New Carden), and, from the district of Kirkcaldy, that part of the electoral division of Auchtertool which lies within the Gray Park polling district. The Council has its headquarters at Dunfermline.

The Council has been re-granted the arms matriculated by the Royal burgh of Dunfermline in 1909. These are clearly based on the device on an old burgh seal of which an early sixteenth century impression is on record.[8] The tower is Malcolm's Tower, a fortress of King Malcolm III (1057–1093), husband of Queen Margaret; some remains of it can still be seen in Pittencrieff Glen. The red windows and portcullis denote its Royal ownership and the lions supporting it are considered to be Royal lions. The Latin Motto – "May the rock be inaccessible" – appears to recall that Malcolm's Tower was built on a site "strikingly adapted for a stronghold".[9]

6

LOTHIAN REGION

The LOTHIAN Region consists of the county of the city of Edinburgh, the county of East Lothian, the county of Midlothian (except the electoral division of Heriot & Stow in the district of Gala Water), and the county of West Lothian (except the burgh of Bo'ness and the district of Bo'ness). The Region is divided into four Districts: West Lothian, City of Edinburgh, Midlothian, and East Lothian.

LOTHIAN
REGIONAL COUNCIL

Azure, a saltire Argent, surmounted at the fess point by an inescutcheon Gules, fimbriated Or, and charged with a sun in splendour Or, a bordure counter-compony of the First and Second.

Above the Shield is placed a coronet appropriate to a statutory Region, *videlicet*:– a circlet richly chased, from which are issuant four thistles leaved (one and two halves visible) Or; and on a Compartment below the Shield are set for *Supporters*, dexter, a lion rampant Vert, armed and langued Gules, and sinister, a unicorn Argent, armed, maned and unguled Or, and gorged with a collar Gules, from which is pendant an oval badge Azure, fimbriated Or, charged with a saltire Argent.

(Lyon Register lix, 57: 7 May 1976)

LOTHIAN REGIONAL COUNCIL has its headquarters at Edinburgh.

The Council's arms follow the basic Regional design of a St Andrew's cross within a blue and silver bordure and surmounted by a red inescutcheon with a gold fimbriation. The inescutcheon is charged with a golden sun in splendour, a feature taken from the arms of the Earldom of Lothian. The dexter supporter is a green lion, which comes from the arms of Midlothian County Council, and the sinister supporter is the unicorn common to all the Regional Councils' coats of arms.

WEST LOTHIAN DISTRICT COUNCIL

Azure, issuant from a mount in base, an oak tree fructed all Or, a bordure Argent charged with four gillyflowers Gules, alternately with as many laurel leaves slipped Vert.

Above the Shield is placed a coronet appropriate to a statutory District, *videlicet*:— a circlet richly chased, from which are issuant eight thistle-heads (three and two halves visible) Or.

(Lyon Register lix, 10: 27 March 1975)

WEST LOTHIAN DISTRICT COUNCIL administers an area comprising (1) the following parts of the county of West Lothian: the burghs of Armadale, Bathgate, Linlithgow, and Whitburn, the districts of Linlithgow, Torphichen & Bathgate, Uphall, Whitburn & Livingston, and the electoral divisions of Abercorn, Winchburgh East and Winchburgh West, from the district of Kirkliston & Winchburgh, and (2) the districts of East Calder and West Calder in the county of Midlothian. The Council's headquarters are at Bathgate.

The Council has been allowed to take over the arms granted to West Lothian County Council in 1952. They show the coat borne, for their Earldom, on an inescutcheon *en surtout* of their shield, by the Livingstone Earls of Linlithgow, but four of the red gillyflowers on the bordure have been replaced by green laurel leaves, thus giving a reference to the Hope Earls and Marquesses of Linlithgow, who have a green bay leaf in the centre of their arms.

CITY OF EDINBURGH DISTRICT COUNCIL administers an area comprising (1) the county of the city of Edinburgh, (2) the burgh of Queensferry and the district of Kirkliston & Winchburgh (except the electoral divisions of Abercorn, Winchburgh East and Winchburgh West), in the county of West Lothian, and (3) in the county of Midlothian, the district of Currie and the parish of Cramond. The Council's headquarters are at Edinburgh.

The Council has been allowed to take over the arms matriculated by the city and Royal burgh of Edinburgh in 1732, with the addition of a District Council coronet. These resemble, but are not identical to, the device on the earliest known seals of the

CITY OF EDINBURGH DISTRICT COUNCIL

Argent, a castle triple-towered and embattled Sable, masoned of the First and topped with three fans Gules, windows and portcullis shut of the Last, situate on a rock Proper.

Above the Shield is placed a coronet appropriate to a statutory District, *videlicet*:– a circlet richly chased, from which are issuant eight thistle-heads (three and two halves visible) Or; and on a Wreath of the Colours is set for *Crest* an anchor wreathed about with a cable all Proper; and in an Escrol over the same this *Motto* "Nisi Dominus Frustra"; and on a Compartment below the Shield are set for *Supporters*, on the dexter, a maid richly attired with her hair hanging down her shoulders, and on the sinister, a doe, Proper.

(Lyon Register lix, 1 : 21 January 1975)

city of which fourteenth and fifteenth century impressions are on record. The first example of the arms on a shield is dated 1496 and appears on a seal of St Giles' Church.[1] The principal charge is Edinburgh Castle on its rock; the red windows, fans and portcullis denote that it is a Royal castle but the reason for the silver and black colours is not known. The anchor crest now refers to the maritime associations of the District Council; previously it is said to have referred to the *ex-officio* title of Admiral of the Forth held by the Lord Provost of the city. The dexter supporter may be a Pictish princess in reference to the legend that in ancient days, during a battle, the Pictish kings used to shut up their daughters inside the Castle for safety – hence Edinburgh's former name "Castrum Puellarum; alternatively, as Lord Lyon Balfour Paul has suggested, she may be "simply emblematical of the fair beauty of the city itself".[2] The sinister supporter is the doe of St Giles, the patron saint of Edinburgh. The Latin Motto is an abridgement of Psalm 127: 1, "Except the Lord keep the city, the watchman waketh but in vain".

MIDLOTHIAN DISTRICT COUNCIL

Or, a lion rampant Vert, armed and langued Gules, surmounted of a fess Azure charged with three suns in their splendour of the field.

Above the Shield is placed a coronet appropriate to a statutory District, *videlicet*:– a circlet richly chased, from which are issuant eight thistle-heads (three and two halves visible) Or.

(Lyon Register lix, 49: 27 February 1976)

MIDLOTHIAN DISTRICT COUNCIL administers an area in the county of Midlothian consisting of the burghs of Bonnyrigg & Lasswade, Dalkeith, Loanhead, and Penicuik, the districts of Gala Water (except the electoral division of Heriot & Stow), Lasswade, Musselburgh (except the parish of Inveresk), Newbattle, and Penicuik. The Council's headquarters are at Dalkeith.

The Council has been re-granted the arms granted to Midlothian County Council in 1951. In these the green lion on the gold field refers to the old arms of the Viscountcy of Primrose, now held by the Earls of Rosebery and Midlothian; "Vert, a lion rampant Or" was a coat of augmentation granted to Sir Archibald Primrose of Carrington (grandfather of the 1st Viscount Primrose) by King Charles II as a mark of favour for his loyalty.[3] The gold suns on the blue fess allude to the first and third quarters of the arms of the Earldom of Lothian, now held by the Marquess of Lothian; this was a coat of augmentation assumed by Sir William Kerr, son of the 1st Earl of Ancrum, when he was created Earl of Lothian in 1631.[4]

EAST LOTHIAN DISTRICT COUNCIL

Gules, three bars Ermine, over all a lion rampant Or, armed and langued Azure.

Above the Shield is placed a coronet appropriate to a statutory District, *videlicet*:– a circlet richly chased, from which are issuant eight thistle-heads (three and two halves visible) Or.

(Lyon Register lix, 32: 25 August 1975)

EAST LOTHIAN DISTRICT COUNCIL administers an area comprising the county of East Lothian, and the burgh of Musselburgh, and the parish of Inveresk in the district of Musselburgh, in the county of Midlothian. Its headquarters are at Haddington.

The Council has been allowed to take over the arms granted to East Lothian County Council in 1927. They are of great beauty and simplicity. The red and ermine field comes from the arms of the Giffords of Yester, a family granted lands in East Lothian by King William the Lion (1165–1214) and now represented by the Marquess of Tweeddale. While the lion could recall the King, since the County buildings occupy a site said to have been that of his palace at Haddington, it was chosen in reference to the ancient Earldom of Dunbar, the celebrated East Lothian family of Maitland of Lethington, the Earls of Wemyss & March (the 11th Earl was Lord Lieutenant in 1927), and Sir Archibald Buchan Hepburn (County Convener in 1927), since a lion rampant appears in all of their coats of arms.

7

CENTRAL REGION

The CENTRAL Region consists of (1) the county of Clackmannan, (2) the burghs of Callander, Doune, and Dunblane, the Western district (except the electoral division of Ardoch) and the parish of Muckhart from the Central district, in the county of Perth, (3) the county of Stirling (except the burgh of Kilsyth, the Western No. 3 district, and, from the Central No. 2 district, the electoral division of Kilsyth West and the polling district of Kilsyth East (Banton)), and (4) in the county of West Lothian, the burgh of Bo'ness and the district of Bo'ness. The Region is divided into three Districts: Clackmannan, Stirling, and Falkirk.

CENTRAL REGIONAL COUNCIL

Azure, a saltire Argent, surmounted at the fess point by an inescutcheon Gules, fimbriated Or, and charged with two caltraps in chief and a dexter mailed gauntlet paleways in base all Or, a bordure counter-compony of the First and Second.

Above the Shield is placed a coronet appropriate to a statutory Region, *videlicet*:– a circlet richly chased, from which are issuant four thistles leaved (one and two halves visible) Or; and on a Compartment below the Shield are set for *Supporters*, dexter, a goshawk Proper, and sinister, a unicorn Argent, armed, maned and unguled Or, and gorged with a collar Gules, from which is pendant an oval badge Azure, fimbriated Or, charged with a saltire Argent.

(Lyon Register lix, 45: 26 January 1976)

CENTRAL REGIONAL COUNCIL has its headquarters at Stirling.
The Council's arms follow the basic Regional design of a St Andrew's cross within

a blue and silver bordure surmounted by a red inescutcheon with a gold fimbriation. The inescutcheon is charged with a caltrap (or cheval trap) taken from the arms of Drummond, the main family of the part of Perthshire included in the Region, and from the arms of Stirling County Council, where it recalls the Scottish victory at Bannockburn in 1314; in base is a gauntlet or mannan in reference to the county of Clackmannan. The dexter supporter is a goshawk recalling the falcon crest of the Drummonds, and the sinister supporter is the unicorn common to all the Regional Councils' coats of arms.

CLACKMANNAN DISTRICT COUNCIL

Or, a saltire Gules; a chief, tierced per pale, in the 1st, Vert, a sinister gauntlet, and in the 3rd, also Vert, a dexter gauntlet, both Proper, and in the 2nd, Argent, a pale Sable.

Above the Shield is placed a coronet appropriate to a statutory District, *videlicet*:– a circlet richly chased, from which are issuant eight thistle-heads (three and two halves visible) Or; and in an Escrol under the Shield this *Motto* "Look Aboot Ye".

(Lyon Register lix, 9: 20 January 1975)

CLACKMANNAN DISTRICT COUNCIL administers an area comprising the county of Clackmannan and the parish of Muckhart from the Central district, in the county of Perth. Its headquarters are at Alloa.

The Council has been re-granted the arms granted to Clackmannan County Council in 1927. These show the red saltire on a gold field used by Bruce of Annandale and by Bruce of Clackmannan. This, the gauntlets and the motto recall a legend which tells how King Robert I, when on a visit to Clackmannan, left his glove (mannan) on a stone (clack), and how when he sent his squire to fetch it, the latter said "Look aboot ye here till I return"; ever since the place has been known as Look-Aboot-Ye Brae. The green field in the chief is for agriculture and the black pale on the silver ground recalls the long connection with the District of the Erskine family, as represented by the Earls of Mar & Kellie.

STIRLING DISTRICT COUNCIL

Azure, on a saltire between two caltraps in chief and base and as many spur rowels in the flanks Argent, a lion rampant Gules, armed and langued of the First.

Above the Shield is placed a coronet appropriate to a statutory District, *videlicet*:– a circlet richly chased, from which are issuant eight thistle-heads (three and two halves visible) Or.

(Lyon Register lix, 24: 24 June 1975)

STIRLING DISTRICT COUNCIL administers an area comprising (1) the burghs of Callander, Doune, and Dunblane, and the Western district (except the electoral division of Ardoch), in the county of Perth, and (2) in the county of Stirling, the burghs of Bridge of Allan and Stirling, and the districts Central No. 1, Western No. 1, and Western No. 2. The Council's headquarters are at Stirling.

The Council has been allowed to take over the arms granted to Stirling County Council in 1890. In these the shield and saltire of Scotland have been used as a basis and to them have been added two caltraps (cheval traps) and two spur rowels to recall the famous Scottish victory at Bannockburn near Stirling in 1314; in the battle King Robert I successfully used caltraps to prevent the approach of the English cavalry. The Scottish lion has been added at the centre of the saltire to indicate the close association of Stirlingshire with the Royal House of Scotland.

FALKIRK DISTRICT COUNCIL administers an area comprising (1) the following parts of the county of Stirling: the burghs of Denny & Dunipace, Falkirk, and Grangemouth, the districts Eastern No. 1, Eastern No. 2, Eastern No. 3, Central No. 2 (except the electoral division of Kilsyth West and the polling district of Kilsyth East (Banton)), and (2) in the county of West Lothian, the burgh of Bo'ness and the district of Bo'ness. The Council's headquarters are at Falkirk.

The quartered arms show features from the arms of the four burghs of the District. In the first quarter, for Falkirk (arms matriculated 1906), appear the black field and gold billets of Callendar, the historic family associated with the area from early times and whose estates passed into the Livingstone family after the War of Independence in the fourteenth century; the bend has been made embattled to denote the Roman Wall of Antonine which passed close to the town. The second quarter, for Grangemouth (arms matriculated 1930), shows a stag's head with a cross-crosslet between its antlers

FALKIRK DISTRICT COUNCIL

Quarterly: 1st, Sable, a bend bretessed accompanied by six billets Or, three in chief and three in base; 2nd, Gules, a stag's head erased with a cross-crosslet fitchée between the attires Or; 3rd, per pale Gules and Sable, in a sea in base undy Argent and Azure, a three-masted ship of the 17th century Or, in full sail Proper, flagged Gold; 4th, per fess engrailed Azure and Vert, in chief a demi-angel Proper, attired Argent, wings displayed Or and celestially crowned of the Last, holding in either hand a palm branch of the Second, and in base a bend wavy of the Third charged with a bendlet wavy of the First.

Above the Shield is placed a coronet appropriate to a statutory District, *videlicet*:– a circlet richly chased, from which are issuant eight thistle-heads (three and two halves visible) Or; and in an Escrol under the Shield this *Motto* "Ane for A'".

(Lyon Register lix, 55: 15 April 1976)

thus recalling the town's connections through Abbots Kerse with Holyrood Abbey, which once held the Lordship of Kerse, and with the Bellenden family who were granted it, as part of the Barony of Broughton, after the Reformation. The third quarter is for Bo'ness, properly Borrowstounness (arms matriculated 1930); the red half of the field recalls the long connection of the Dukes of Hamilton with the town and the black half is for the coal-mining industry; the ship, in full sail to denote prosperity, refers to the town's shipping interests, and recalls that in the eighteenth century, Bo'ness was the third seaport in Scotland. The fourth quarter, for Denny & Dunipace (arms granted 1956), shows the angel of peace placed above the bridge over the river Carron which flows between Denny and Dunipace. The angel of peace is an appropriate symbol for the town since the neighbourhood is said to have been the setting for three important treaties in Scottish history and Dunipace takes its name from two ancient mounds nearby – the Hills of Dunipace, which George Buchanan calls "Duni Pacis" or "hills of peace".[1] The Scots Motto recalls "Touch Ane Touch A'", one of the mottoes of the burgh of Falkirk.

8

BORDERS REGION

The BORDERS Region consists of the county of Berwick, the county of Peebles, the county of Roxburgh, the county of Selkirk, and the electoral division of Heriot & Stow from the district of Gala Water in the county of Midlothian. The Region is divided into four Districts: Tweeddale, Ettrick & Lauderdale, Roxburgh, and Berwickshire.

BORDERS REGIONAL COUNCIL

Azure, a saltire Argent, surmounted at the fess point by an inescutcheon Gules, fimbriated Or, and charged with four barrulets wavy Argent between in chief a salmon naiant and in base a ram's head cabossed Proper, a bordure counter-compony of the First and Second.

Above the Shield is placed a coronet appropriate to a statutory Region, *videlicet*:– a circlet richly chased, from which are issuant four thistles leaved (one and two halves visible) Or; and on a Compartment below the Shield are set for *Supporters*, dexter, a Border Knight wearing thigh boots Sable spurred Or, a breastplate and helmet Proper, girt with a sword, his dexter arm flexed at the elbow, the hand grasping a spear paleways also Proper, and sinister, a unicorn Argent, armed, maned and unguled Or, and gorged with a collar Gules, from which is pendant an oval badge Azure, fimbriated Or, charged with a saltire Argent.

(Lyon Register lix, 22: 3 February 1976)

BORDERS REGIONAL COUNCIL has its headquarters at Newtown St. Boswells.

The Council's arms follow the basic Regional design of a St Andrew's cross within a blue and silver bordure and surmounted by a red inescutcheon with a gold fimbriation. The wavy barrulets on the inescutcheon denote the river Tweed – they are four in number as there are four Districts in the Borders Region; the salmon and the ram's head represent its fishing, agricultural and woollen manufacturing interests. The dexter supporter is one of the famous Border knights, and the sinister supporter is the unicorn common to all the Regional Councils' coats of arms.

TWEEDDALE DISTRICT COUNCIL

Quarterly: 1st, Sable, five fraises Argent; 2nd, Azure, a horse's head couped Argent; 3rd, Vert, a golden fleece; 4th, Or, fretty Gules, a chief embattled of the Last charged with two thunderbolts of the First.

Above the Shield is placed a coronet appropriate to a statutory District, *videlicet*:– a circlet richly chased, from which are issuant eight thistle-heads (three and two halves visible) Or; and in an Escrol under the same this *Motto* "Onward Tweeddale".

(Lyon Register lix, 44: 21 October 1975)

TWEEDDALE DISTRICT COUNCIL administers an area comprising the county of Peebles. Its headquarters are at Peebles.

The Council has been allowed to take over the arms granted to Peebles County Council in 1931, but without the supporters and crest. The first quarter has five silver fraises (or cinquefoils) on a black field in reference to the Frasers of Oliver Castle, one of the most famous and most ancient families of Tweeddale; from this family, whose arms are said to have been "Sable, six cinquefoils Argent",[1] are descended by marriage the Hays of Yester, Marquesses of Tweeddale, who also bear silver cinquefoils (on a blue field) in their arms. The second quarter shows the arms of Horsbrugh, a family whose connection with Tweeddale is almost as old as that of the Frasers. In the third quarter there is a golden fleece on a green field to represent the District's staple industries, agriculture, sheep-farming and woollen manufacturing. The fourth quarter shows the arms of Thorburn of Glenormiston; Mr M. G. (later Sir Michael) Thorburn was Lord Lieutenant and Convener of the County in 1931. The Motto needs no explanation.

ETTRICK & LAUDERDALE
DISTRICT COUNCIL

Argent, on a mount in base a stag lodged reguardant in front of
an oak tree, all Proper, the tree charged of an inescutcheon of
the arms of the Earl of Lauderdale, *videlicet*:– Or, a lion rampant
Gules couped at all his joints of the field, within the Royal Tressure Azure.

Above the Shield is placed a coronet appropriate to a statutory
District, *videlicet*:– a circlet richly chased, from which are issuant
eight thistle-heads (three and two halves visible) Or; and in an
Escrol under the Shield this *Motto* "Leal to the Border".

(Lyon Register lix, 35: 9 September 1975)

ETTRICK & LAUDERDALE DISTRICT COUNCIL administers an area
comprising (1) the county of Selkirk, (2) the burgh of Lauder and the West district
(except the electoral divisions of Gordon, Hume & Nenthorn, and Westruther), in the
county of Berwick, (3) the electoral division of Heriot & Stow from the district of Gala
Water in the county of Midlothian, and (4) in the county of Roxburgh, the burgh of
Melrose and the district of Melrose (except that part of the parish of Roxburgh which
lies within this district). The Council's headquarters are at Galashiels.

The arms are based on those granted to Selkirk County Council in 1927. They
show a stag at rest in Ettrick Forest, a favourite Royal hunting ground. The device has
had a long association with Selkirkshire and was used by the Selkirkshire Volunteers;
there is an example on a regimental medal, dated 1807, which is in the Scottish United
Services Museum in Edinburgh Castle. It is also said to have been connected with Sir
Walter Scott who refers to it and to the motto in a letter of 1827, addressed to the
Friendly Society of Selkirk, whose flag he had been asked to design.[2] To the Selkirkshire
arms (which represent Ettrick) has been added an inescutcheon bearing the arms of
Maitland, Earl of Lauderdale, to represent Lauderdale. The County Council's motto,
which appears on the 1807 medal, has been retained.

ROXBURGH DISTRICT COUNCIL administers an area comprising (1) the
burghs of Hawick, Jedburgh, and Kelso, the districts of Hawick, Jedburgh, and Kelso,
and that part of the parish of Roxburgh which lies within the district of Melrose, all in
the county of Roxburgh, and (2) the parish of Nenthorn in the county of Berwick. The
Council has its headquarters at Hawick.

The Council has been allowed to take over the arms of Roxburgh County Council
without the crest. Originally granted to the county of Roxburgh in 1798, very little
seems to have been recorded about them, but they appear to have had associations with

ROXBURGH DISTRICT COUNCIL

Azure, a unicorn saliant Argent, horned, maned and un-guled Or, the tail tufted of the Last; on a chief of the Second a hunting horn Sable, stringed and viroled Gules, between two esquires' helmets of the field.

Above the Shield is placed a coronet appropriate to a statutory District, *videlicet*:– a circlet richly chased, from which are issuant eight thistle-heads (three and two halves visible) Or; and in an Escrol under the Shield this *Motto* "Ne Cede Malis Sed Contra Audentior Ito".

(Lyon Register lix, 16: 6 May 1975)

Local Defence Forces, as an example of them appears on a fragment of an 1804 Colour of the Kelso Volunteers which is preserved in Kelso Old Parish Church. Any attempt at explanation must, however, be largely conjectural.

The unicorn appears in the arms of Kerr, Duke of Roxburghe, and Kerr Marquess of Lothian, and seems to have been a symbol long connected with Roxburghshire. The helmets and the hunting horn almost certainly represent the famous Border riders, one of whom appears in the arms of the Royal burgh of Jedburgh (matriculated 1680), and their rallying-cry "A-Henwoody, A-Henwoody" which "when once raised, made every heart burn with ardour, and every hand grasp a weapon, and every foot hasten to the Henwood",[3] an old forest which probably extended from Oxnam to the river Jed. The Latin Motto – "Yield not to evil things but rather go on more boldly" – is a quotation from Virgil, *Aeneid*, vi., 95; its sentiments are similar to those expressed in the mottoes of well-known Border families, but its choice may have been inspired by the words "Nec Aspera Terrent" (the motto of the Hanoverian Order of Guelph) which have a long connection with the famous Scottish regiment, the King's Own Scottish Borderers (formed in 1782).

BERWICKSHIRE DISTRICT COUNCIL administers an area in the county of Berwick comprising the burghs of Coldstream, Duns, and Eyemouth, the East and Middle districts, and the electoral divisions of Gordon and Westruther and the parish of Hume, from the West district. The Council's headquarters are at Duns.

The Council has been re-granted the arms granted to Berwick County Council in 1890. They show a bear chained to a wych-elm, this being a punning reference to the name Berwick (Bear wyck). Legends tell that in olden times Berwickshire was covered by forest and that many bears lived there. The coat of arms symbolises how the bears

BERWICKSHIRE DISTRICT
COUNCIL

Argent, on a mount Vert, a bear Sable, collared and chained Or, standing in front of a tree Proper.

Above the Shield is placed a coronet appropriate to a statutory District, *videlicet*:– a circlet richly chased, from which are issuant eight thistle-heads (three and two halves visible) Or.

(Lyon Register lix, 40: 12 November 1975)

were brought under subjection after the building of Berwick Castle. It closely resembles the ancient arms of the borough of Berwick-upon-Tweed (recorded at Lyon Office in 1958) and has obviously had a long association with Berwickshire.

9

STRATHCLYDE REGION

The STRATHCLYDE Region consists of (1) the county of the city of Glasgow, (2) the county of Bute, (3) the county of Dunbarton, (4) the county of Lanark, (5) the county of Renfrew, (6) the county of Argyll (except the district of Ardnamurchan and the electoral divisions of Ballachulish and Kinlochleven from the district of North Lorn, (7) the county of Ayr, and (8) in the county of Stirling, the burgh of Kilsyth, the Western No. 3 district, and from the Central No. 2 district, the electoral division of Kilsyth West and the polling district of Kilsyth East (Banton). The Region is divided into nineteen Districts: Argyll & Bute, Dumbarton, City of Glasgow, Clydebank, Bearsden & Milngavie, Strathkelvin, Cumbernauld & Kilsyth, Monklands, Motherwell, Hamilton, East Kilbride, Eastwood, Lanark, Renfrew, Inverclyde, Cunninghame, Kilmarnock & Loudoun, Kyle & Carrick, and Cumnock & Doon Valley.

STRATHCLYDE REGIONAL COUNCIL has its headquarters at Glasgow.
The Council has not registered arms but uses a non-heraldic device consisting of an outline map of Scotland on which the area of the Strathclyde Region is specially marked. This device appears on the Council's seal.

ARGYLL & BUTE DISTRICT COUNCIL

Parted per fess and in chief per pale: 1st, gyronny of eight Or and Sable; 2nd, Or, a wing displayed Gules, claw membered Sable, grasping a sword in pale Azure, hilted and pommelled Argent and environed of an antique crown also Gules; in base Or, a lymphad, oars in action, sails furled Sable, at the masthead a beacon enflamed Gules; over all a bar chequy Azure and Argent.

Above the Shield is placed a coronet appropriate to a statutory District, *videlicet*:– a circlet richly chased, from which are issuant eight thistle-heads (three and two halves visible) Or; and in an Escrol under the same this *Motto* "Seas Ar Coir".

(Lyon Register lix, 54: 20 May 1976)

ARGYLL & BUTE DISTRICT COUNCIL administers an area comprising (1) the following parts of the county of Argyll: the burghs of Campbeltown, Dunoon, Inveraray, Lochgilphead, Oban, and Tobermory, the districts of Cowal, Islay, Jura & Colonsay, Kintyre, Mid Argyll, Mull, North Lorn (except the electoral divisions of Ballachulish and Kinlochleven), South Lorn, and Tiree & Coll, and (2) the burgh of Rothesay and the district of Bute, in the county of Bute. The Council's headquarters are at Lochgilphead.

The arms combine the main features of the arms granted to Argyll County Council in 1953 along with a blue/silver chequy on a bar in reference to Bute. The Argyll features are in chief (1) the black and gold gyronny of the Campbell, Dukes of Argyll and (2) a displayed wing with a claw, a very early heraldic device which is used here to represent the Macdonald eagle, along with a sword and a crown for the southern part of the Lordship of the Isles. In base is the black galley of the Lordship of Lorn with four oars visible and with the flaming beacon at its masthead – this Lordship has been held by the Earls and Dukes of Argyll since the fifteenth century. The Stewart chequy on the bar recalls the many Royal and other Stewart links with Bute. The Gaelic Motto – "Maintain Our Right" – was used by Argyll County Council.

DUMBARTON DISTRICT COUNCIL

Azure, an elephant statant Argent, tusked Or, charged on the forehead with a crescent Gules, bearing on his back a tower Proper.

Above the Shield is placed a coronet appropriate to a statutory District, *videlicet*:– a circlet richly chased, from which are issuant eight thistle-heads (three and two halves visible) Or; and in an Escrol under the same this *Motto* "Aonaichte".

(Lyon Register lix, 62: 25 July 1977)

DUMBARTON DISTRICT COUNCIL administers an area in the county of Dunbarton comprising the burghs of Dumbarton, Cove & Kilcreggan, and Helensburgh, the districts of Helensburgh and Vale of Leven, and the electoral divisions of Bowling and Dunbarton from the district of Old Kilpatrick. The Council has its headquarters at Dumbarton.

The arms follow closely those matriculated by the Royal burgh of Dumbarton in c.1673. They show an elephant with a tower on its back, a device which appeared on an ancient burgh seal of which a 1357 impression is on record.[1] The elephant has been blazoned "statant" and not "passant" (as it was (rather inaccurately) in the burgh arms) and its forehead bears a red crescent for difference, thus indicating that it is "a second happening". It is said to have been chosen originally because in shape it was thought to resemble Dumbarton Rock; the tower on its back is for Dumbarton Castle. The Gaelic Motto – "Togetherness" – refers to the union, in the District, of the three burghs and part of the county.

CITY OF GLASGOW DISTRICT COUNCIL

Argent, on a mount in base Vert an oak tree Proper, the stem at the base thereof surmounted by a salmon on its back also Proper, with a signet ring in its mouth Or, on the top of the tree a redbreast and in the sinister fess point an ancient hand bell both also Proper.

Above the Shield is placed a coronet appropriate to a statutory District, *videlicet:*– a circlet richly chased, from which are issuant eight thistle-heads (three and two halves visible) Or; and on a Wreath of the Colours is set for *Crest* the half length figure of Saint Kentigern affrontée vested and mitred, his right hand raised in the act of benediction, and having in his left hand a crosier all Proper; and on a Compartment below the Shield, inscribed of this *Motto* "Let Glasgow Flourish", are set for *Supporters* two salmon Proper each holding in its mouth a signet ring Or.

(Lyon Register lix, 3: 6 February 1975)

CITY OF GLASGOW DISTRICT COUNCIL administers an area comprising the county of the city of Glasgow, and the following parts of the county of Lanark: the burgh of Rutherglen, from the Eighth district the electoral divisions of Bankhead, Cambuslang Central, Cambuslang North, Hallside, Rutherglen, and those parts of the electoral divisions of Cambuslang South and Carmunnock which lie outwith the area of East Kilbride New Town, and, from the Ninth district, the electoral divisions of Baillieston, Garrowhill, Mount Vernon & Carmyle, and Springboig. The Council has its headquarters at Glasgow.

The Council has been re-granted the arms matriculated by the city and Royal burgh of Glasgow in 1866, minus the helmet and mantling, and with the addition of the District Council coronet. The charges on the shield have been associated with the city since the thirteenth and fourteenth centuries and recall three legendary miracles performed by St Kentigern (or Mungo), the city's patron saint. The tree, traditionally a hazel tree, recalls how he produced fire from a hazel branch; the redbreast recalls the robin he restored to life; the salmon and the ring recall his intervention to help the Queen of Cadzow who was suspected of unfaithfulness by her husband. The hand bell is his much venerated bell (c.f. Lanark District Council). The colours seem to have no special significance; at one time the field appears to have been "parted per fess Argent and Gules" and is so shown on the mace of Glasgow University. The salmon supporters refer to the legend mentioned above and could also allude to the river Clyde and salmon-fishing, which was the city's staple industry in the eighteenth century. The crest is St Mungo himself – but without a halo – thus harking back to a city seal dated 1268. The Motto is a shortened version of "Lord, Let Glasgow Flourish by the Preaching of Thy Word and the Praising of Thy Name".[2]

CLYDEBANK DISTRICT COUNCIL

Argent, a saltire Gules, in chief a cog-wheel Sable, in fess dexter a demi-figure of Saint Patrick Proper, in fess sinister a representation of part of the Antonine Wall Proper, and in base, upon the waves of the sea, a lymphad, sails furled, oars in action of the Third, flagged of the Second.

Above the Shield is placed a coronet appropriate to a statutory District, *videlicet*:– a circlet richly chased, from which are issuant eight thistle-heads (three and two halves visible) Or; and in an Escrol under the Shield this *Motto* "Labore et Scientia".

(Lyon Register lix, 33: 3 September 1975)

CLYDEBANK DISTRICT COUNCIL administers an area in the county of Dunbarton comprising the burgh of Clydebank and the district of Old Kilpatrick (except the electoral divisions of Bowling, Dunbarton, and that part of the electoral division of Hardgate which lies within the parish of New Kilpatrick). Its headquarters are at Clydebank.

The arms granted to the Council are similar in design to those matriculated by the burgh of Clydebank in 1930, but four of the charges have been changed. The red saltire on the silver field is for Lennox, in which province the District lies; as it is also a St Patrick's cross, it is doubly appropriate since parts of the parishes of Old and New Kilpatrick are within the District. The cog-wheel symbolises all the local industries and the demi-figure of St Patrick refers to Old Kilpatrick, a burgh of barony from 1672,[3] and where the saint is reputed to have been born. A representation of part of the Roman Antonine's Wall has been included as the Wall and Roman forts at Old Kilpatrick and Greenhill are features common to the burgh and to the villages in the District. The lymphad is for Clyde shipbuilding. The Latin Motto – "By Work and by Knowledge" – was the motto of the burgh of Clydebank.

BEARSDEN & MILNGAVIE
DISTRICT COUNCIL

Per pale: dexter, per bend Gules and Sable a bear's head couped Argent, langued of the First, muzzled Azure; sinister, quarterly of the Third and Second a cross moline, square pierced of the field and divided per cross of the First and Or; on a chief enarched per pale of the Last and Third a bar wavy of the Fourth, over all at the middle chief a rose of the First, barbed and seeded Proper.

Above the Shield is placed a coronet appropriate to a statutory District, *videlicet*:– a circlet richly chased, from which are issuant eight thistle-heads (three and two halves visible) Or; and in an Escrol under the same this *Motto* "Bear The Gree".

(Lyon Register lix, 47: 9 January 1976)

BEARSDEN & MILNGAVIE DISTRICT COUNCIL administers an area in the county of Dunbarton comprising the burghs of Bearsden and Milngavie, and from the district of Old Kilpatrick, that part of the electoral division of Hardgate which lies within the parish of New Kilpatrick. The Council's headquarters are at Bearsden.

The arms show features from the arms granted to the burgh of Bearsden in 1959 and from those of the burgh of Milngavie (matriculated 1938). The dexter side, for Bearsden, shows a bear looking into his den, thus making a direct reference to the town's name; the red colour is for Lennox and St Patrick, since Bearsden is in New Kilpatrick parish. The sinister side, for Milngavie, shows a square-pierced cross moline, to represent a mill-rind, since it is somewhat similar in form to the iron fitting set in the netherstone of a mill; in addition, the quartered background gives a kind of rotatory effect and thus could be said to denote the mill-wheel. All this alludes to Gavie's Mill from which the town may get its name. The red and silver colours recall the Earls of Lennox to whom the lands of Milngavie belonged before they passed to the Grahams, Earls and Dukes of Montrose. It was the Grahams who founded Gavie's Mill and this family connection is indicated by the black and gold colours. The rose in chief, the Lennox rose, appeared in the arms of both burghs; the bar wavy is for the Allander water, the local river. The Scots Motto means "Have the first place"; it comes from Robert Burns' song "A Man's a Man for a' that", and was the motto of the burgh of Bearsden.

STRATHKELVIN DISTRICT COUNCIL administers an area comprising (1) the burgh of Kirkintilloch and those parts of the electoral divisions of Twechar and Waterside in the district of Kirkintilloch & Cumbernauld which lie outside the designated area of Cumbernauld New Town, all in the county of Dunbarton, (2) the burgh of Bishopbriggs and the electoral divisions of Chryston and Stepps from the Ninth dis-

STRATHKELVIN DISTRICT COUNCIL

Per pale: dexter, per fess Sable and bendy Or and Vert, in chief an episcopal mitra pretiosa of the Second stoned and jewelled Proper; sinister, Azure, a wall towered and embattled Argent, in the port Sable a portcullis Or, standing upon a mount Proper, in chief three stars of five points Or; over all on a chief Argent, a barrulet wavy Azure.

Above the Shield is placed a coronet appropriate to a statutory District, *videlicet*:– a circlet richly chased, from which are issuant eight thistle-heads (three and two halves visible) Or; and in an Escrol under the Shield this *Motto* "Progress with Vigilance".

(Lyon Register lix, 28: 11 June 1976)

trict, in the county of Lanark, and (3) the Western No. 3 district in the county of Stirling. The Council's headquarters are at Kirkintilloch.

The arms which have been granted to the Council contain the main features of the arms of the burgh of Kirkintilloch (matriculated 1938) and those of the burgh of Bishopbriggs (granted 1964). The dexter side, for Bishopbriggs, shows a richly jewelled mitre for the Bishops and Archbishops of Glasgow and the gold/green pattern denotes the "riggs" which once belonged to them; the mitre is set on a black field to recall the local connection with Stirling of Cadder (now represented by Stirling of Keir). The sinister side, for Kirkintilloch, shows a towered wall to represent the Roman fort (on Antonine's Wall) which formerly stood on Peel Hill in the town; the Council specially asked for a portcullis to be included. In the chief the gold and blue colours of the Comyns appear as they were the Superiors of the burgh in the thirteenth century. The three stars are said to refer to the town's ecclesiastical connections and to the symbolism of the triad (connected with the Holy Trinity) and the pentalpha (five-pointed stars which refer to the wounds of Christ): they are symbolic of health and strength.[4] The chief overall is for the river Kelvin and its strath. The Motto is conventional but recalls "Ca' Canny but Ca' Awa'" used by the burgh of Kirkintilloch.

CUMBERNAULD & KILSYTH DISTRICT COUNCIL administers an area comprising (1) the burgh of Cumbernauld, and from the district of Kirkintilloch & Cumbernauld, the electoral division of Croy & Dullatur and those parts of the electoral divisions of Twechar and Waterside which lie within the designated area of Cumbernauld New Town, all within the county of Dunbarton, and (2) in the county of Stirling, the burgh of Kilsyth, and the electoral division of Kilsyth West and the polling district of Kilsyth East (Banton) from Central No. 2 district. The Council's headquarters are at Cumbernauld.

CUMBERNAULD & KILSYTH DISTRICT COUNCIL

Azure, on a saltire Argent cantoned between in chief a bull's head cabossed Argent armed Or, in base a plate fimbriated Or and charged with two barrulets wavy Azure, in the dexter flank two shuttles in saltire Or, garnished with thread Argent, and in sinister flank a miner's lamp Argent, enflamed Proper, an open Bible Proper, binding and fore-edges Gules.

Above the Shield is placed a coronet appropriate to a statutory District, *videlicet*:– a circlet richly chased, from which are issuant eight thistle-heads (three and two halves visible) Or; and in an Escrol under the Shield this *Motto* "Daur and Prosper".

(Lyon Register lix, 36: 8 October 1975)

By special request of the Council, the arms have as their main feature the Scottish saltire on its blue field. The bull's head recalls the famous Cumbernauld wild white cattle;[5] what was their habitation is now the Council's Palacerigg Country Park. The plate in base with its two wavy lines denotes that Cumbernauld is situated on the water-sheds of the rivers Forth and Clyde. The shuttles and the miner's lamp come from the arms of the burgh of Kilsyth (granted 1972) and allude to the District's associations with weaving and coal and ironstone mining. The open Bible also comes from the Kilsyth arms and refers to local associations with the Covenanters. The Scots Motto was used by the burgh of Cumbernauld (arms granted 1969).

MONKLANDS DISTRICT COUNCIL administers an area in the county of Lanark comprising the burghs of Airdrie and Coatbridge, the Ninth district (except the electoral divisions of Baillieston, Chryston, Garrowhill, Mount Vernon & Carmyle, Springboig, and Stepps), and the electoral division of Shottskirk in the Seventh district. The Council has its headquarters at Coatbridge.

The arms recall those of the two burghs and the county with which the District is associated. In dexter chief appear the arms of Airdrie (matriculated 1930), based on those of Aitcheson of Rochsolloch, the family who were the Superiors of the town from 1769 to 1824. In sinister chief are the arms of Coatbridge (matriculated 1930), where the black field and the flaming tower, which represents a blast furnace, stand for the iron and steel industry. In base the two pierced silver cinquefoils on a red field (for Hamilton) come from the arms of Lanark County Council (originally granted to the Commissioners of Supply for Lanarkshire in 1886); they are accompanied by a Cistercian monk to recall that the lands of Monkland were once owned by the Cistercian Abbey of

MONKLANDS DISTRICT COUNCIL

Per fess wavy, in chief per pale Or and Sable, and in base Gules:
1st, a double-headed eagle displayed Sable, beaked and membered Gules, in chief a crescent between two spur rowels Vert;
2nd, a tower Argent masoned Sable, windows and port Gules,
from the battlements flames issuant Proper; 3rd, between two
cinquefoils Argent pierced of the field the figure of a Cistercian
monk affrontée habited Proper.

Above the Shield is placed a coronet appropriate to a statutory
District, *videlicet*:– a circlet richly chased, from which are issuant
eight thistle-heads (three and two halves visible) Or; and in an
Escrol under the Shield this *Motto* "Vigilanter".

(Lyon Register lix, 25: 18 July 1975)

Newbattle in East Lothian. The wavy division of the shield alludes to the Monkland
canal. The Latin Motto – "Watchfully" – recalls the mottoes of Airdrie and the County
Council.

MOTHERWELL DISTRICT COUNCIL

Per fess Gules and Sable, in chief two cinquefoils Ermine and
in base a well Proper.

Above the Shield is placed a coronet appropriate to a statutory
District, *videlicet*:– a circlet richly chased, from which are
issuant eight thistle-heads (three and two halves visible) Or;
and in an Escrol under the same this *Motto* "Industria".

(Lyon Register lix, 46: 30 September 1976)

MOTHERWELL DISTRICT COUNCIL administers an area comprising the
burgh of Motherwell & Wishaw, the Sixth district (except the electoral divisions of
Bothwell & Uddingston South and Uddingston North), and the Seventh District

(except the electoral division of Shottskirk), all in the county of Lanark. The Council's headquarters are at Motherwell.

The arms are the same (less supporters) as those matriculated by the burgh of Motherwell & Wishaw in 1930. The two ermine cinquefoils on the red field denote the close connections of the District with the Lords Hamilton of Dalzell. The black field is for coal-mining while the well (or fountain) recalls the ancient Lady's Well (dedicated to the Virgin Mary), from which the town of Motherwell may have got its name. The Latin Motto – "Industry" – comes from the seal of the former burgh of Wishaw (united with Motherwell in 1920).

HAMILTON DISTRICT COUNCIL

Gules, a fess embattled and enarched Argent, masoned Sable, between three cinquefoils pierced of the Second.

Above the Shield is placed a coronet appropriate to a statutory District, *videlicet*:– a circlet richly chased, from which are issuant eight thistle-heads (three and two halves visible) Or; and in an Escrol under the Shield this *Motto* "Virtue and Vigilance".

(Lyon Register lix, 30: 12 August 1975)

HAMILTON DISTRICT COUNCIL administers an area comprising the following parts of the county of Lanark: the burgh of Hamilton, the Fourth district (except the electoral division of Avondale), the electoral divisions of Bothwell & Uddingston South and Uddingston North from the Sixth district, and, from the Eighth district, the electoral divisions of Blantyre and Stonefield, and that part of High Blantyre electoral division lying outwith the designated area of East Kilbride New Town. The Council's headquarters are at Hamilton.

The Council's arms show the arms of the burgh of Hamilton (matriculated 1886) differenced by an embattled and enarched fess. The burgh coat was based on a version of the Hamilton family arms reputed to have been given to it by Anne, Duchess of Hamilton, in whose favour it was created a burgh of regality in 1669;[6] the arms show cinquefoils which are pierced, and they are in silver instead of ermine. The fess has been added to represent Bothwell Brig, the oldest bridge in Lanarkshire, dating from 1486.[7] The Motto was a local suggestion from a competition; it echoes the "Sola Nobilitat Virtus" of Hamilton burgh and the "Vigilantia" of Lanark County Council.

EAST KILBRIDE
DISTRICT COUNCIL

Per fess, in chief Gules and in base per pale Or and
Vert, a cross flory of the Second between two mullets
Argent in chief and an oystercatcher bird Proper in
base; a chief chequy per pale, dexter, Argent and
Azure, sinister, Argent and Sable; all within a bordure
Gules.

Above the Shield is placed a coronet appropriate to a
statutory District, *videlicet*:– a circlet richly chased,
from which are issuant eight thistle-heads (three and
two halves visible) Or; and in an Escrol under the
Shield this *Motto* "Prosper but Dreid".

(Lyon Register lix, 23: 24 June 1975)

EAST KILBRIDE DISTRICT COUNCIL administers an area in the county of
Lanark comprising the burgh of East Kilbride, the electoral division of Avondale from
the Fourth district, and, from the Eighth district, those parts of the electoral divisions of
High Blantyre, Cambuslang South and Carmunnock which lie within the designated
area of East Kilbride New Town. The Council has its headquarters at East Kilbride.
    The Council has been allowed to take over the arms granted to the burgh of East
Kilbride in 1963, with the addition of a red bordure for difference. At the top of the
shield is a Stewart silver/blue chequy to recall Stewart of Torrance, balanced by a
chequy in silver and black to recall Maxwell of Calderwood; both these families have a
long connection with the District. The cross flory is for the church (of St Bride) which
gives the town its Gaelic name, while the silver stars on the red field refer to the Lindsays of Dunrod who lived at Mains Castle and were the Superiors of most of the surrounding country until the seventeenth century. In the base is an oystercatcher, the
bird always associated with St Bride; it stands on a background of gold, for the industry
and wealth of the District, and green for its former rural surroundings. The Motto is
derived from the "Live but Dreid" used by the Lindsays, as now represented by the
Earls of Lindsay.

    EASTWOOD DISTRICT COUNCIL administers an area comprising the First
district in the county of Renfrew. Its headquarters, temporarily at Paisley, are to be
moved to Giffnock in due course.
    The arms have as their main feature a wood of oak trees charged with an Eastern
crown, to denote Eastwood; oak trees were chosen because it is recorded that in 1812 the
prevailing trees in the Eastwood area were birch, alder, ash and oak.[8] In the chief reference is made to three families closely connected with the District:– the fleur-de-lis is for

EASTWOOD DISTRICT COUNCIL

Argent, issuant from a mount in base, a wood of oak trees fructed Proper, charged with an eastern crown Or; on a chief wavy Azure, on a pale of the First a saltire Sable charged in the centre with a hedgehog of the Second, in dexter chief a fleur-de-lis of the Last, and in sinister chief a cross-crosslet fitchée issuant from a crescent of the First.

Above the Shield is placed a coronet appropriate to a statutory District, *videlicet*:– a circlet richly chased, from which are issuant eight thistle-heads (three and two halves visible) Or.

(Lyon Register lix, 38: 17 October 1975)

the Montgomeries, who held the baronies of Eastwood and Eaglesham, the black saltire with its hedgehog is for the Maxwells of Caerlaverock, who held the barony of Mearns, and the silver cross-crosslet and crescent represent Cathcart of Cathcart. The wavy line is for the river Cart.

LANARK DISTRICT COUNCIL

Tierced in pairle reversed: 1st, Or, an eagle with two heads displayed Sable, armed and membered Gules, holding in his dexter claw an ancient hand bell Proper; 2nd, Gules, a goat's head erased Argent, armed Or; 3rd, Argent, a man's heart Gules, imperially crowned Proper.

Above the Shield is placed a coronet appropriate to a statutory District, *videlicet*:– a circlet richly chased, from which are issuant eight thistle-heads (three and two halves visible) Or; and in an Escrol under the same this *Motto* "Let the Deed Shaw".

(Lyon Register lix, 31: 12 August 1975)

LANARK DISTRICT COUNCIL administers an area comprising the burghs of Biggar and Lanark, and the First, Second and Third districts, in the county of Lanark. Its headquarters are at Lanark.

The tierced-in-pairle design of the arms was specially chosen because it was used in the arms of the burgh of Biggar (matriculated 1930) and because it was similar to the division "per chevron" of the arms of Lanark County Council. The double-headed eagle comes from the arms of the Royal burgh of Lanark (matriculated 1929) and is thought to be a Roman eagle; there were several Roman camp sites in the vicinity. The ancient hand bell is for St Kentigern (or Mungo), who was Lanark's patron saint (cf. City of Glasgow District Council). The device of the eagle and the hand bell can be traced back to a burgh seal impression dated 1357.[9] The goat's head comes from the arms of the burgh of Biggar and, being the Fleming crest, recalls the long connection between that family and the town. The crowned heart of Douglas refers to the long association of that famous family with the District and also recalls the uncrowned heart in the arms of Lanark County Council. The Scots Motto is that of Fleming and of the burgh of Biggar; according to tradition, the words "Let the deed shaw" were said by Sir Robert Fleming to Robert Bruce (later King Robert I), after the latter had killed John Comyn of Badenoch (the Red Comyn) in Greyfriars church in Dumfries in 1306.

RENFREW DISTRICT COUNCIL

Azure, a lymphad, sails furled Argent, on a shield Or pendant from the mast a fess chequy of the First and Second.

Above the Shield is placed a coronet appropriate to a statutory District, *videlicet*:– a circlet richly chased, from which are issuant eight thistle-heads (three and two halves visible) Or.

(Lyon Register lix, 56: 30 September 1976)

RENFREW DISTRICT COUNCIL administers an area comprising the burghs of Barrhead, Johnstone, Paisley, and Renfrew, and the Second, Third, and Fourth districts, in the county of Renfrew. It has its headquarters at Paisley.

The Council has been allowed to take over the arms (minus crest and motto) of Renfrew County Council (originally granted to the Commissioners of Supply for Renfrewshire in 1889). The blue/silver fess on the gold field and the ship combine the coat of the High Stewards of Scotland, whose first abode in Scotland was Renfrewshire, and thus the Royal House of Stewart, with the galley of the West of Scotland and of the Royal burgh of Renfrew (arms matriculated 1676).

INVERCLYDE DISTRICT COUNCIL

Or, on a base barry wavy Azure and Argent, a three-masted ship in full sail Proper, having for figurehead a lion rampant Gules, flying from the foremast and mizzenmast a streamer Gules, and from the main mast and jackstaff the banner of Scotland *viz.*, Azure, a saltire Argent; in chief between two mullets of six points Sable pierced of the field, a hurt charged with a covered cup of the First.

Above the Shield is placed a coronet appropriate to a statutory District, *videlicet*:– a circlet richly chased, from which are issuant eight thistle-heads (three and two halves visible) Or; and in an Escrol under the Shield this *Motto* "Meliora Semper Prospicimus".

(Lyon Register lix, 50: 9 March 1976)

INVERCLYDE DISTRICT COUNCIL administers an area in the county of Renfrew comprising the burghs of Gourock, Greenock, and Port Glasgow, and the Fifth district. Its headquarters are at Greenock.

The arms have a sailing ship as their main feature as such vessels appear the arms of the burghs of Gourock (granted 1954), Greenock (matriculated 1923) and Port Glasgow (matriculated 1929); in the last two cases they are set on gold fields. The red lion figurehead comes from the Port Glasgow arms. In chief appear two black mullets from the arms of Burns of Wemyss, Baron Inverclyde, and a covered cup within a blue roundel to recall the family of Shaw of Greenock. The Latin Motto – "We look forward to better things" – was a local suggestion.

CUNNINGHAME DISTRICT COUNCIL administers an area comprising (1) the following parts of the county of Ayr: the burghs of Ardrossan, Irvine, Kilwinning, Largs, Saltcoats, and Stevenston, the districts of Irvine, Kilbirnie, and West Kilbride, and those parts of the designated area of Irvine New Town within the districts of Ayr and Kilmarnock, and (2) in the county of Bute, the burgh of Millport and the districts of Arran and Cumbrae. The Council has its headquarters at Irvine.

The arms have as their main feature a black Cunningham shakefork on its silver field; it is said that this family "being by office Masters of the King's Stables and Horses, took for their armorial figure the instrument whereby hay is thrown up to horses, which in blazon is called a shakefork".[10] In the dexter flank appear the arms of the Royal burgh of Irvine (matriculated 1927) which display the crest of the Kings of Scotland, a crowned lion sitting on a crown and holding the sword and sceptre; there is an impression dated 1680 of the reverse of the oldest known burgh seal which shows such a device.[11] The right to use the Royal crest is said to have been granted to the citi-

CUNNINGHAME DISTRICT COUNCIL

Argent, a shakefork Sable cantoned between in chief a leopard's head affrontée holding in its mouth a weaver's shuttle Proper, in the dexter flank on an imperial crown Or a lion sejant affrontée Azure imperially crowned Gold holding in his dexter paw a sword and in his sinister a sceptre both Proper, and in the sinister flank a lymphad Gules, mast, rigging and sails furled Proper, flagged Or.

Above the Shield is placed a coronet appropriate to a statutory District, *videlicet*:– a circlet richly chased, from which are issuant eight thistle-heads (three and two halves visible) Or; and in an Escrol under the Shield this Motto "Sense and Worth".

(Lyon Register lix, 66: 27 January 1979)

zens of Irvine by King Robert I because of special services they had rendered to him. The ship in the sinister flank symbolises generally the maritime associations of the District. In chief the leopard's head with the weaver's shuttle refers to the main industry of the inland parts of the District, Beith, Dalry and Kilbirnie. This heraldic charge is symbolic of weaving; it is common to the arms of all the societies and incorporations of weavers that have recorded arms in Scotland and also appears in the arms granted in 1487 to the Worshipful Company of Weavers of London.[12] The Motto was a local choice.

KILMARNOCK & LOUDOUN DISTRICT COUNCIL administers an area in the county of Ayr comprising the burghs of Darvel, Galston, Kilmarnock, Newmilns & Greenholm, and Stewarton, and the district of Kilmarnock (except that part of the designated area of Irvine New Town which lies within this district). The Council's headquarters are at Kilmarnock.

The Council has not registered arms and at present uses a plain seal and a non-heraldic device which shows the letters KL with a symbolic coronet above and a squirrel in the foreground. The arms of the burgh of Kilmarnock (matriculated 1929) had squirrels for supporters.

KYLE & CARRICK DISTRICT COUNCIL administers an area comprising the following parts of the county of Ayr: the burghs of Ayr, Girvan, Maybole, Prestwick, and Troon, the districts of Ayr, (except that part of the designated area of Irvine New Town which lies within this district), Girvan, and Maybole, and from the district of Dalmellington, that part of the parish of Ayr within this district and the polling district of Coylton. The Council has its headquarters at Ayr.

KYLE & CARRICK
DISTRICT COUNCIL

Per pale Or and Argent: dexter, issuant from a fess chequy Azure and Argent a demi-lion rampant Gules; sinister, a chevron of the Last.

Above the Shield is placed a coronet appropriate to a statutory District, *videlicet:*– a circlet richly chased, from which are issuant eight thistle-heads (three and two halves visible) Or; and in an Escrol under the Shield this *Motto* "Forward as One".

(Lyon Register lix, 42: 28 November 1975)

The arms show, on the dexter side, for Kyle, a red demi-lion rising from a Stewart blue/silver fess; this is taken from a seal used in 1369 by John Stewart, Lord of Kyle (later King Robert III).[13] The sinister side, for Carrick, shows the red chevron on its silver field of the ancient Earldom of Carrick. The Motto is conventional.

CUMNOCK & DOON VALLEY
DISTRICT COUNCIL

Per fess wavy, a barrulet wavy Azure; in chief per pale Gules and Argent, a demi-lion rampant issuant counter-changed Argent and Azure; in base Or, on a mound Vert, a pine tree fructed Proper between dexter, a lozenge Sable and sinister, a garb Gules banded Argent; all within a bordure per pale Argent and Gules charged with eight roses counterchanged, barbed and seeded Vert.

Above the Shield is placed a coronet appropriate to a statutory District, *videlicet:*– a circlet richly chased, from which are issuant eight thistle-heads (three and two halves visible) Or; and in an Escrol under the same this *Motto* "We Serve".

(Lyon Register lix, 18: 20 August 1976)

CUMNOCK & DOON VALLEY DISTRICT COUNCIL administers an area in the county of Ayr comprising the burgh of Cumnock & Holmhead, and the districts of

Cumnock and Dalmellington (except that part of the parish of Ayr which lies within this district and the polling district of Coylton). The Council has its headquarters at Cumnock.

The arms show in chief and on the bordure the main features of the arms granted to the burgh of Cumnock & Holmhead in 1959. These recall the Dunbar and Crichton connections with the town. Surrounded by a bordure of eight roses, recalling a similar feature in the Dunbar arms, they show a demi-lion rampant which is half silver on a red field (for Dunbar) and half blue on a silver field (for Crichton). The wavy barrulet is for the river Doon and in the base the black lozenge, the pine tree and the garb respectively represent coal mining, forestry and agriculture, the main industries of the Doon Valley. The Motto is conventional.

10

DUMFRIES & GALLOWAY REGION

The DUMFRIES & GALLOWAY Region consists of the county of Dumfries, the county of Kirkcudbright, and the county of Wigtown. It is divided into four Districts: Wigtown, Stewartry, Nithsdale, and Annandale & Eskdale.

DUMFRIES & GALLOWAY REGIONAL COUNCIL

Azure, a saltire Argent, surmounted at the fess point by an inescutcheon Gules, fimbriated Or, and charged with a lion rampant Argent crowned Or, a bordure counter-compony of the First and Second.

Above the Shield is placed a coronet appropriate to a statutory Region, *videlicet*:– a circlet richly chased, from which are issuant four thistles leaved (one and two halves visible) Or; and on a Compartment below the Shield are set for *Supporters*, dexter, a stag Proper, and sinister, a unicorn Argent, armed, maned and unguled Or, and gorged with a collar Gules, from which is pendant an oval badge Azure, fimbriated Or, charged with a saltire Argent.

(Lyon Register lix, 21 : 17 July 1975)

DUMFRIES & GALLOWAY REGIONAL COUNCIL has its headquarters at Dumfries.

The Council's arms follow the basic Regional design of a St Andrew's cross within a blue and silver bordure and surmounted by a red inescutcheon with a gold fimbriation. The inescutcheon is charged with the crowned silver lion of Galloway. The dexter supporter, a stag, comes from the arms of Maxwell, Earl of Nithsdale, where it appears both as supporter and crest; the sinister supporter is the unicorn common to all the Regional Councils' coats of arms.

WIGTOWN DISTRICT COUNCIL

Per pale indented: dexter Azure, a lion rampant Argent, armed and langued Gules, crowned with an antique crown Or and gorged of an antique crown Vert; sinister, Gules, a chevron Argent and issuing from the sinister chief a quadrant of the sun arrayed Or; on a chief Azure, having a fillet Ermine, a saltire Or charged with nine lozenges also Azure.

Above the Shield is placed a coronet appropriate to a statutory District, *videlicet*:– a circlet richly chased, from which are issuant eight thistle-heads (three and two halves visible) Or.

(Lyon Register lix, 29: 21 July 1975)

WIGTOWN DISTRICT COUNCIL administers an area comprising the county of Wigtown, and the Western district (except the electoral division of Anwoth & Girthon) in the county of Kirkcudbright. Its headquarters are at Stranraer.

The Council has been allowed to take over the arms granted in 1955 to Wigtown County Council. On the dexter side appears the crowned silver lion of Galloway on its blue field; the lion wears an antique crown as a collar and thus recalls not only the Douglas Lords of Galloway but also the historic family of Macdouall. On the sinister there is the silver chevron on a red field of Fleming, Earl of Wigtown, with a sunburst from the seal of the Royal burgh of Wigtown in the top sinister corner. In the chief the nine blue lozenges on the gold saltire recall a similar device (with the colours reversed) in the arms of Dalrymple, Earl of Stair. The saltire in the chief and the chevron also recall the Agnews of Lochnaw, in whose arms these ordinaries appear. The chief is separated from the rest of the shield by a distinctive ermine fillet; the use of a fur acknowledges that each of the three compartments of the arms is derived from the arms of a Peerage House.

STEWARTRY DISTRICT COUNCIL administers an area in the county of Kirkcudbright comprising the burghs of Castle Douglas, Dalbeattie, Gatehouse-of-Fleet, Kirkcudbright, and New Galloway, the districts of Castle Douglas, Dalbeattie, Glenkens, and Kirkcudbright, and, from the Western district, the electoral division of Anwoth & Girthon. The Council's headquarters are at Kirkcudbright.

The Council has been re-granted the arms granted to Kirkcudbright County Council in 1951. They show the crowned lion of Galloway on its blue field. The silver/

green chequy of the bar denotes the checked tablecloth used by the Stewards of the Lords of Galloway when collecting taxes and other dues, thus recalling that this part of Galloway is still known as the Stewartry of Kirkcudbright.

STEWARTRY DISTRICT COUNCIL

Azure, a lion rampant Argent, armed and langued Gules, crowned with an antique crown Or surmounted of a bar chequy Argent and Vert.

Above the Shield is placed a coronet appropriate to a statutory District, *videlicet*:– a circlet richly chased, from which are issuant eight thistle-heads (three and two halves visible) Or.

(Lyon Register lix, 15: 2 April 1975)

NITHSDALE DISTRICT COUNCIL administers an area comprising the burghs of Dumfries and Sanquhar, and the districts of Dumfries (except the parishes of Dalton and Lochmaben), Thornhill and Upper Nithsdale, all in the county of Dumfries, and the Eastern district in the county of Kirkcudbright. The Council has its headquarters at Dumfries.

NITHSDALE DISTRICT COUNCIL

Argent, a double-headed eagle displayed Sable, beaked and membered Gules, surmounted of an escutcheon of the First charged with a saltire of the Second and surcharged in the centre with a hurcheon Or, within a bordure of the Third charged with five estoiles of the Fourth; on a chief wavy Azure, an endorse of the Fourth between dexter, the demi-figure of the Archangel Michael, wings expanded, brandishing in his dexter hand a sword all Proper and on his sinister arm an escutcheon of the First charged with a cross of the Third; and sinister, on a rock in base Proper, a double-leaved gate of the Third, triple-towered, on an ascent of five steps flanked by two towers all of the First, towers arch-roofed and masoned of the Second, vanes of the Third.

Above the Shield is placed a coronet appropriate to a statutory District, *videlicet*:– a circlet richly chased, from which are issuant eight thistle-heads (three and two halves visible) Or; and in an Escrol under the Shield this *Motto* "Reviresco".

(Lyon Register lix, 20: 23 September 1976)

The arms show (1) St Michael, the patron saint of Dumfries, taken from the arms of the Royal burgh of Dumfries (matriculated 1931) – a representation of the saint appears on a burgh seal of which a fourteenth century impression is on record;[1] (2) from the arms of the Royal burgh of Sanquhar (matriculated 1929), the old castle of Sanquhar, first the seat of the Rosses and then of the Crichtons of Sanquhar; the five steps leading up to the gate recall the Five Incorporated Trades of the burgh whose arms were based on an old burgh seal of which an impression dated 1732 is on record;[2] (3) the arms of Maxwell, Earl of Nithsdale (of the Herries branch), showing a double-headed eagle with a shield on its breast bearing a black saltire charged with the gold hedgehog of Herries; the stars on the bordure recall the field "semée of estoiles Or" in the arms of the Royal burgh of Dumfries. The wavy chief denotes the river Nith. The Latin Motto – "I flourish again" – was that of the Maxwell Earls of Nithsdale and was used by the burgh of Maxwelltown (united with Dumfries in 1931).

ANNANDALE & ESKDALE DISTRICT COUNCIL

Or, on a saltire Gules a golden fleece of the First; on a chief of the Second a bar wavy Argent charged with two barrulets wavy Azure.

Above the Shield is placed a coronet appropriate to a statutory District, *videlicet*:– a circlet richly chased, from which are issuant eight thistle-heads (three and two halves visible) Or; and in an Escrol under the same this *Motto* "Quinque Uniter".

(Lyon Register lix, 48: 13 February 1976)

ANNANDALE & ESKDALE DISTRICT COUNCIL administers an area comprising the following parts of the county of Dumfries: the burghs of Annan, Langholm, Lochmaben, Lockerbie, and Moffat, the districts of Annan, Gretna, Langholm, Lockerbie, and Moffat, and the parishes of Dalton and Lochmaben from the district of Dumfries. The Council's headquarters are at Annan.

The Council's arms are very reminiscent of those matriculated by the Royal burgh of Annan in 1918. They show the arms of Bruce, Lord of Annandale, "Or, a saltire and a chief Gules," to which has been added a golden fleece from the arms of the burgh of Langholm (matriculated 1930) to represent Eskdale. The two blue barrulets on the silver wavy bar on the chief are for the rivers Annan and Esk. The Latin Motto – "Five in Unity" – recalls that five burghs are joined together in the District.

11

ISLANDS AREAS

There are three Islands Areas, Orkney, Shetland, and Western Isles.

ORKNEY ISLANDS COUNCIL

Parted per pale Azure and Gules: in the dexter a dragon galley Or, sails furled Argent, and in the sinister a lion rampant imperially crowned Or, armed and langued Azure, holding in its forepaws a battle axe erect in pale Gold.

Above the Shield is placed a coronet appropriate to a statutory Islands Area, *videlicet*:– a circlet richly chased, from which are issuant four dolphins two and two respectant naiant embowed (two visible) Or; and on a Compartment below the Shield, with this *Motto* "Boreas Domus Mare Amicus", are set for *Supporters*, dexter, a udaller habited of the fifteenth century, and sinister, a unicorn Argent, armed, maned and unguled Or, and gorged with a collar Gules, from which is pendant an oval badge Azure, fimbriated Or, charged with a saltire Argent.

(Lyon Register lix, 11 : 3 March 1975)

ORKNEY ISLANDS COUNCIL administers an area comprising the county of Orkney. Its headquarters are at Kirkwall.

The Council has been allowed to take over the arms granted in 1931 to Orkney County Council, with a change in the sinister supporter. They show, on the dexter side, the gold galley on a blue field of the ancient Earldom of Orkney, and on the sinister, the crowned golden lion on a red field from the Royal arms of Norway, recalling that Norway was once Norwegian territory. The battle-axe held by the lion has been coloured gold for difference. The arms are partly based on an old seal of the Communitas Orcadiae of which a 1425 impression is on record showing the Norwegian Royal arms with two men as supporters;[1] it is of interest to note that Orkney was one of only two Norwegian provinces which had been allowed to use the arms of their king on their seals and that the supporters, once thought to be udallers, may instead represent the medieval Orkney aristocracy – "the best men" – who controlled the law courts.[2] The Latin Motto – "The North our home, the sea our friend" – was chosen in 1931. The dexter supporter is a udaller, a term which, under the udal system of land tenure which still applies in Orkney and Shetland, covers the whole of the land-owning class and he is appropriately dressed in his "braws" (best clothes) for the important task of supporting the Council's arms. The sinister supporter is the unicorn common to all the Islands Councils' coats of arms.

SHETLAND ISLANDS COUNCIL

Azure, a base invected barry Argent and Sable, the alternate party lines being engrailed and plain, a dragon ship Or, the sail charged with a raven Proper, oars in action Or, flag and mast Gules.

Above the Shield is placed a coronet appropriate to a statutory Islands Area, *videlicet*:– a circlet richly chased, from which are issuant four dolphins two and two respectant naiant embowed (two visible) Or; and on a Compartment below the Shield, with this *Motto* "Med Lögum Skal Land Byggja", are set for *Supporters*, dexter, a Shetland pony Proper, and sinister, a unicorn Argent, armed, maned and unguled Or, and gorged with a collar Gules, from which is pendant an oval badge Azure, fimbriated Or, charged with a saltire Argent.

(Lyon Register lix, 19: 17 June 1975)

SHETLANDS ISLANDS COUNCIL administers an area comprising the county of Zetland. Its headquarters are at Lerwick.

The arms are based on those granted to Zetland County Council in 1956. They show a Viking warship, recalling the old link with Norway and Denmark. The ship and its oars are coloured gold and set on a blue field since these were the colours of the ancient Earldom (or Jarldom) of Orkney of which the Shetlands were once part. This Earldom in 1379 passed into the family of Sinclair (or St Clair) of Roslin, as heirs by marriage of the Norse Jarls, and so the sea has been coloured silver and black and given an engrailed pattern in reference to them. The sail of the dragon ship has been spread as in the arms of the burgh of Lerwick (matriculated 1882) and bears the raven which was the burgh's crest and was also the badge of the Jarls. The Motto, in Old Norse, was used by Zetland County Council: it comes from a speech in *Njal's Saga* (Chapter 70) and means "By law shall the land be built up". The dexter supporter is one of Shetland's famous ponies, and the sinister supporter is the unicorn common to all the Islands Councils' coats of arms.

WESTERN ISLES ISLANDS COUNCIL

Or, on a fess wavy Azure between three lymphads, oars in action, sails furled Sable, flagged Gules, two barrulets wavy Argent.

Above the Shield is placed a coronet appropriate to a statutory Islands Area, *videlicet*:— a circlet richly chased, from which are issuant four dolphins two and two respectant naiant embowed (two visible) Or; and on a Compartment below the Shield, with this *Motto* "Ardaichidh Fireantachd Cinneach", are set for *Supporters*, dexter, a golden eagle Proper, and sinister, a unicorn Argent, armed, maned and unguled Or, and gorged with a collar Gules, from which is pendant an oval badge Azure, fimbriated Or, charged with a saltire Argent; and for *Badge* a lymphad, sail furled, oars in action, surmounting a circlet Sable.

(Lyon Register lix, 51; 9 September 1976)

WESTERN ISLES ISLANDS COUNCIL administers an area comprising (1) the districts of Barra, Harris, North Uist and South Uist, in the county of Inverness, and (2) the burgh of Stornoway and the district of Lewis, in the county of Ross & Cromarty. Its headquarters are at Stornoway.

The arms show three black galleys on a gold field and thus refer back to the arms of the Lordship of the Isles: "Or, an eagle displayed Gules, surmounted with a galley Sable". The wavy fess and the barrulets denote the sea. The Gaelic Motto means

"Righteousness exalteth a nation" and comes from Proverbs 14:34. The dexter supporter, a golden eagle, is typical of the area and also recalls the eagle in the arms of the Lordship of the Isles; the sinister supporter is the unicorn common to all the Islands Councils' coats of arms. The Council also applied for and was granted a Badge: a black galley on a circlet of the same colour. This is the first example of the granting of a badge to a Scottish Local Authority.

The Letters Patent granting the arms were issued in both English and Gaelic.

APPENDIX I

ARRANGEMENT OF LOCAL GOVERNMENT IN SCOTLAND PRIOR TO 16 MAY 1975

Counties	Burghs	Districts
Zetland*	Lerwick†	Bressay; Burra Isle; Delting; Dunrossness; Fetlar; Gulberwick & Quarff; Nesting & Lunnasting; Northmavine; Sandsting & Aithsting; Tingvall; Unst; Walls & Sandness; Whalsay & Skerries; Yell
Orkney*	Kirkwall†; Stromness	Eday; Hoy & Walls; Mainland; North Ronaldshay; Rousay; Sanday; Shapinsay; South Ronaldshay; Stronsay; Westray & Papa Westray
Caithness*	Wick†; Thurso†	Central; Eastern; Northern; Southern; Western
Sutherland*	Dornoch†	Assynt; Dornoch & Creich; Eddrachillis & Durness; Golspie, Rogart & Lairg; Kildonan, Loth & Clyne; Tongue & Farr
Ross & Cromarty*	Tain†; Dingwall†; Fortrose†; Cromarty†; Invergordon†; Stornoway†	Avoch; Dingwall; Fearn; Fortrose; Gairloch‡; Invergordon; Lewis; Lochbroom; Lochcarron; Muir of Ord; South Uist; Tain
Inverness*	Inverness†; Fort William†; Kingussie	Aird; Badenoch; Barra; Harris; Inverness; Lochaber; North Uist; Skye; South Uist
Nairn*	Nairn†	Nairn
Moray*	Elgin†; Forres†; Burghead†; Grantown-on-Spey†; Lossiemouth & Branderburgh; Rothes†	Cromdale; Duffus & Drainie; Elgin; Fochabers; Forres; Rothes & Knockando

Counties	Burghs	Districts
Banff*	Banff†; Cullen†; Aberchirder; Aberlour; Buckie†; Dufftown†; Findochty; Keith†; Macduff†; Portknockie†; Portsoy†	Aberchirder; Banff; Buckie; Cullen; Dufftown; Keith
Aberdeen*	Kintore†; Inverurie†; Peterhead†; Ballater†; Ellon†; Fraserburgh†; Huntly†; Old Meldrum†; Rosehearty†; Turriff	Aberdeen; Alford; Deer; Deeside; Ellon; Garioch; Huntly; Turriff
Kincardine*	Inverbervie†; Banchory†; Laurencekirk; Stonehaven†	Laurencekirk; Lower Deeside; St Cyrus; Stonehaven; Upper Deeside
Angus*	Montrose†; Brechin†; Arbroath†; Forfar†; Carnoustie†; Kirriemuir†; Monifieth†	Brechin; Carnoustie; Forfar; Kirriemuir; Monifieth; Montrose
Perth*	Perth†; Auchterarder†; Aberfeldy; Abernethy; Alyth†; Blairgowrie & Rattray†; Callander†; Coupar Angus†; Crieff†; Doune†; Dunblane†; Pitlochry†	Central; Eastern; Highland; Perth; Western
Argyll*	Inveraray†; Campbeltown†; Oban†; Dunoon†; Lochgilphead†; Tobermory†	Ardnamurchan; Cowal; Islay; Jura & Colonsay; Kintyre; Mid Argyll; Mull; North Lorn; South Lorn; Tiree & Coll

Counties	Burghs	Districts
Bute*	Rothesay†; Millport	Arran‡; Bute; Cumbrae
Dunbarton*	Dumbarton†; Clydebank†; Cove & Kilcreggan†; Helensburgh†; Kirkintilloch†; Milngavie†; Bearsden†; Cumbernauld†	Helensburgh; Kirkintilloch & Cumbernauld; Old Kilpatrick; Vale of Leven
Stirling*	Stirling†; Falkirk†; Bridge of Allan; Denny & Dunipace†; Grangemouth†; Kilsyth†;	Central No. 1; Central No. 2; Eastern No. 1; Eastern No. 2; Eastern No. 3; Western No. 1; Western No. 2; Western No. 3
Clackmannan*	Alloa†; Alva; Dollar; Tillicoultry	Alloa; Hillfoots
Kinross*	Kinross†	—
Fife*	St Andrews†; Kirkcaldy†; Cupar†; Kilrenny, Anstruther Easter & Anstruther Wester†; Burntisland†; Inverkeithing†; Kinghorn†; Pittenweem†; Dunfermline†; Crail†; Culross†; Auchtermuchty†; Elie & Earlsferry†; Falkland†; Newburgh†; Buckhaven & Methil; Cowdenbeath†; Ladybank; Leslie†; Leven†; Lochgelly†; Markinch†; Newport-on-Tay†; St Monance†; Tayport†	Cupar; Dunfermline; Glenrothes; Kirkcaldy; Lochgelly; St Andrews; Wemyss

Counties	Burghs	Districts
East Lothian*	Haddington†; Dunbar†; North Berwick†; Cockenzie & Port Seton†; East Linton, Prestonpans; Tranent	Dunbar; Haddington; North Berwick; Prestonpans; Tranent
Midlothian*	Musselburgh†; Bonnyrigg & Lasswade†; Dalkeith†; Loanhead†; Penicuik†	Currie; East Calder; Gala Water; Lasswade; Musselburgh; Newbattle; Penicuik; West Calder
West Lothian*	Linlithgow†; Queensferry†; Armadale†; Bathgate†; Bo'ness†; Whitburn†	Bo'ness & Carriden; Kirkliston & Winchburgh; Linlithgow; Torphichen & Bathgate; Uphall; Whitburn & Livingston
Lanark*	Lanark†; Rutherglen†; Airdrie†; Coatbridge†; Hamilton†; Biggar†; Motherwell & Wishaw†; East Kilbride†; Bishopbriggs†	First; Second; Third; Fourth; Sixth; Seventh; Eighth; Ninth
Renfrew*	Renfrew†; Greenock†; Paisley†; Port Glasgow†; Barrhead†; Gourock†; Johnstone†	First; Second; Third; Fourth; Fifth

Counties	Burghs	Districts
Ayr*	Ayr†; Irvine†; Kilmarnock†; Ardrossan†; Cumnock & Holmhead†; Darvel†; Galston†; Girvan†; Kilwinning; Largs†; Maybole†; Newmilns & Greenholm†; Prestwick†; Saltcoats†; Stewarton†; Troon†; Stevenston†	Ayr; Cumnock; Dalmellington; Girvan; Irvine; Kilbirnie; Kilmarnock; Maybole; West Kilbride
Wigtown*	Wigtown; Whithorn†; Stranraer†; Newton-Stewart	Machars; Rhins
Kirkcudbright*	Kirkcudbright†; New Galloway†; Castle Douglas†; Dalbeattie†; Gatehouse-of-Fleet†	Castle Douglas; Dalbeattie; Eastern; Glenkens; Kirkcudbright; Western
Dumfries*	Dumfries†; Annan†; Lochmaben†; Sanquhar†; Langholm†; Lockerbie†; Moffat†	Annan; Dumfries; Gretna; Langholm; Lockerbie; Moffat; Thornhill; Upper Nithsdale
Peebles*	Peebles†; Innerleithen†	Broughton; Innerleithen; Linton; Peebles
Selkirk*	Selkirk†; Galashiels†	North; South
Roxburgh*	Jedburgh†; Hawick†; Kelso†; Melrose†	Hawick; Jedburgh; Kelso; Melrose
Berwick*	Lauder†; Coldstream†; Duns†; Eyemouth†	East; Middle; West

COUNTIES OF CITIES	Edinburgh†	—
	Dundee†	—
	Aberdeen†	—
	Glasgow†	—

Notes

* The County Council had recorded arms.
† The Burgh had recorded arms.
‡ The District Council had recorded arms.

ARMS OF THE BURGH OF DOUNE AND PRE-1975 DISTRICT COUNCILS

BURGH OF DOUNE

Or, a fess chequy Azure and Argent, in chief a representation of the Mercat Cross of Doune between two pairs of pistols in saltire muzzles uppermost all Proper, and in base a cushion Gules.

Below the Shield, which is ensigned of a burghal coronet suitable to a Police Burgh (viz., Azure masoned Argent), is placed in an Escrol this *Motto* "Aim True".

(Lyon Register lv, 82: 3 July 1974)

DOUNE was erected into a Burgh of Barony in favour of James Stewart, 3rd Earl of Moray in 1611, but may have been a burgh in 1434–35.[1] It became a Police Burgh in 1890. The arms are appropriately based on those of Stewart with a Moray red cushion added in base. In chief are the main features on the device on the Burgh seal: the Mercat Cross of the Burgh, with a pair of crossed pistols on either side to recall the celebrated Doune pistolmakers of the seventeenth and eighteenth centuries.

ARRAN DISTRICT COUNCIL

Parted per pale engrailed: dexter, parted per fess Gules and Argent, in chief three cinquefoils two and one Ermine and in base a lymphad, sails furled Sable, flagged of the First; sinister, Or, an oak tree Proper surmounted of a fess chequy Azure and Argent.

(Lyon Register l, 16: 15 February 1967)

A differenced version of the arms of Bute County Council (granted 1927) in which there are references to the strong Hamilton and Stewart links with the county. The party line has been made engrailed and an oak tree added in the sinister half of the shield as a special allusion to the close connection with Arran of the Hamilton family.

GAIRLOCH DISTRICT COUNCIL

Argent, on a pale Azure between two laurel leaves slipped Vert, a caberfeidh Or with a cinquefoil of the First between its attires; on a chief engrailed Gules, a pale of the Fourth between two lions rampant of the First, the pale charged of a beacon Azure masoned Argent and enflamed of the Fifth.

(Lyon Register l, 48: 12 July 1968)

A differenced version of the arms of Ross & Cromarty County Council (granted 1957). The party line below the chief has been made engrailed and there has been some rearrangement of the main features – the Ross lions, the MacLeod beacon and the Mackenzie caberfeidh. A silver cinquefoil and two laurel leaves have been added in special reference to the Mackenzies of Gairloch. The beacon has been given special prominence because of the former MacLeod connection with the district.

APPENDIX III
COMMUNITY COUNCILS

Only ten Community Councils have so far recorded arms.

The Royal Burgh of St Andrews Community Council
(North East Fife District)

Parted per pale Azure and Argent: in the dexter, on a mount in base the figure of Saint Andrew Proper bearing his cross in front of him Argent; in the sinister, growing out of a mount in base an oak tree Proper, fructed Or, in front of the trunk a boar passant Sable, langued Gules, armed Or.

Above the Shield is placed a coronet appropriate to a statutory Community Council, *videlicet*:– a circlet richly chased from which are issuant four thistle leaves (one and two halves visible) and four pine cones (two visible) Or; and in an Escrol below the same this *Motto* "Dum Spiro Spero".

(Lyon Register lix, 113: 3 November 1978)

Bathgate Community Council (West Lothian District)

Azure, on a mount between two oak trees a castle triple-towered Proper, an open gate Gules, the main tower charged with the Arms of Fitzalan (*videlicet*:– Gules, a lion rampant Or, armed and langued Argent) and the other two towers with a banner of Scotland (*videlicet*:– Azure, a saltire Argent), in base a loch undy Argent and of the field.

Above the Shield is placed a coronet appropriate to a statutory Community Council, *videlicet*: – a circlet richly chased from which are issuant four thistle leaves (one and two halves visible) and four pine cones (two visible) Or; and in an Escrol below the Shield this *Motto* "Commune Bonum Intra Muros".

(Lyon Register lix, 76 : 1 February 1979)

North Berwick Community Council (East Lothian District)

Azure, upon a sea in base undy Argent and of the First semée of fish Sable and Or respectively, a lymphad of the Second, her jib set and mainsail furled, within her four rowers with oars in action, and seated in the stern an Earl robed and coroneted all Proper, for figurehead a demi-lion rampant Gules, and at the masthead a pennon of the Last charged of Scotland (viz. Azure, a Saint Andrew's cross Argent) in the hoist; in the sinister chief is set the sun in his splendour Or.

Above the Shield is placed a coronet appropriate to a statutory Community Council, *videlicet*:– a circlet richly chased from which are issuant four thistle leaves (one and two halves visible) and four pine cones (two visible) Or; and in an Escrol below the same this *Motto* "Victoriae Gloria Merces".

(Lyon Register lix, 68:15 May 1978)

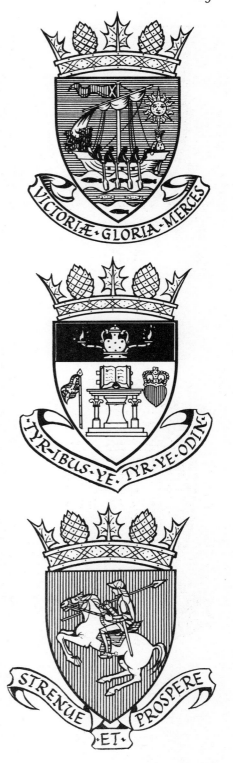

Hawick Community Council (Roxburgh District)

Argent, an altar, thereon an open Bible, both Proper, between on the dexter, a flag Azure charged with a saltire Or and inscribed with the date 1514 Gold, waving towards the dexter from a staff of the Last, and on the sinister a man's heart Gules ensigned with an imperial crown Gold; on a chief Sable, a lamp with two branches also Gold, enflamed and irradiated Proper.

Above the Shield is placed a coronet appropriate to a statutory Community Council, *videlicet*:– a circlet richly chased from which are issuant four thistle leaves (one and two halves visible) and four pine cones (two visible) Or; and in an Escrol below the same this *Motto* "Tyr-ibus Ye Tyr Ye Odin".

(Lyon Register lix, 112: 23 October 1978)

The Royal Burgh of Jedburgh Community Council (Roxburgh District)

Gules, on a horse saliant Argent, furnished Azure, a chevalier armed at all points, grasping in his right hand a kind of lance (called the Jedburgh Staff) Proper.

Above the Shield is placed a coronet appropriate to a statutory Community Council, *videlicet*:– a circlet richly chased from which are issuant four thistle leaves (one and two halves visible) and four pine cones (two visible) Or; and in an Escrol below the same this *Motto* "Strenue et Prospere".

(Lyon Register lix, 76 : 1 February 1979)

Kelso Community Council (Roxburgh District)

Azure, springing from a meadow in base a rose tree in full flower Proper and pendant therefrom, between an eagle and a dove addorsed Argent, an escutcheon charged with the Royal Arms of Scotland, viz. Or, within a double tressure flory and counter-flory, a lion rampant Gules, armed and langued Azure.

Above the Shield is placed a coronet appropriate to a statutory Community Council *videlicet*:– a circlet richly chased from which are issuant four thistle leaves (one and two halves visible) and four pine cones (two visible) Or; and in an Escrol below the same this *Motto* "Dae Richt Fear Nocht".

(Lyon Register lix, 74: 1 February 1979)

Duns Community Council (Berwickshire District)

Parted per pale Argent and Vert: a castle triple-towered per pale Gules and of the First, windows port and turret caps Sable, a bordure parted per pale of the Third and First, charged with four roses barbed and seeded of the Second, alternately with as many escutcheons, all counterchanged; on a canton Or, a cushion of the Third.

Above the Shield is placed a coronet appropriate to a statutory Community Council, *videlicet*:– a circlet richly chased from which are issuant four thistle leaves (one and two halves visible) and four pine cones (two visible) Or; and in an Escrol below the same this *Motto* "Duns Dings A'".

(Lyon Register lix, 100:25 April 1978)

Bishopbriggs Community Council (Strathkelvin District)

Per fess in chief Sable and in base bendy Or and Vert, a fess wavy Argent charged with a barrulet wavy Azure, and in chief an episcopal mitra pretiosa of the Second stoned and jewelled Proper.

Above the Shield is placed a coronet appropriate to a statutory Community Council, *videlicet*:– a circlet richly chased from which are issuant four thistle leaves (one and two halves visible) and four pine cones (two visible) Or; and in an Escrol below the same this *Motto* "God Gie the Gain".

(Lyon Register lix, 75: 13 December 1978)

Biggar Community Council (Lanark District)

Tierced in pairle reversed: 1st, Azure, on a meadow Proper, a plough contournée Argent; 2nd, Azure, on a meadow Proper, a garb Or; 3rd, Gules, a goat's head erased Argent, armed Or.

Above the Shield is placed a coronet appropriate to a statutory Community Council, *videlicet*:– a circlet richly chased from which are issuant four thistle leaves (one and two halves visible) and four pine cones (two visible) Or; and in an Escrol below the Shield this *Motto* "Let the Deed Shaw".

(Lyon Register lix, 96: 12 September 1977)

The Royal Burgh of Lanark Community Council (Lanark District)

Or, an eagle with two heads displayed Sable, armed and membered Gules, holding in his dexter claw an ancient hand bell Proper, in chief a burghal coronet Sable, in the flanches two hounds paleways confrontée Proper, collared of the Third and belled Proper, in the two base points as many fish hauriant addorsed, that on the dexter in bend and that on the sinister in bend sinister, both Proper, holding in their mouths an annulet of the Third.

Above the Shield is placed a coronet appropriate to a statutory Community Council *videlicet*:– a circlet richly chased from which are issuant four thistle leaves (one and two halves visible) and four pine cones (two visible) Or.

(Lyon Register lix, 114:8 November 1978)

For further details see *Scottish Burgh and County Heraldry,* 147–148 (St Andrews), 181 (Bathgate), 169–170 (North Berwick), 237–238 (Hawick), 236–237 (Jedburgh), 238–239 (Kelso), 244 (Duns), 192 (Bishopbriggs), 189–190 (Biggar), and 185–186 (Lanark).

BIBLIOGRAPHY

In the Notes set out below the following bibliographical abbreviations have been used.

Barron, *Regalia*	*In Defence of the Regalia.* Edited by Rev. Douglas G. Barron. London, 1910.
Bain	*Calendar of Documents relating to Scotland 1108–1509.* Edited by Joseph Bain. 4 vols. Edinburgh, 1881–1888.
Buchan, *Peebles-shire*	*A History of Peeblesshire.* Edited by J. W. Buchan and ors. 3 vols. Glasgow, 1925–1927.
Buchanan, *Scotland*	Buchanan, George, *History of Scotland.* A translation and new edition. Edinburgh, 1821.
Burgoyne	Burgoyne, Gerald, *The Fife and Forfar Imperial Yeomanry and its Predecessors.* Cupar-Fife, 1904.
Bute, *RPB*	Bute, John, Marquess of, Macphail, J. R. N., Lonsdale, H. W., *The Arms of the Royal and Parliamentary Burghs of Scotland.* Edinburgh, 1897.
Craig-Brown, *Selkirkshire*	Brown, Thomas Craig-, *The History of Selkirkshire.* 2 vols. Edinburgh, 1886.
Cruickshank	Cruickshank, John, *The Armorial Ensigns of the Royal Burgh of Aberdeen.* Aberdeen, 1888.
Fox-Davies, *Heraldry*	Fox-Davies, A. C., *A Complete Guide to Heraldry.* Revised and annotated by J. P. Brooke-Little. London, 1969.
Fox-Davies, *Public Arms*	Fox-Davies, A. C., *The Book of Public Arms.* 2nd Edition London, 1915.
Henderson, *Dunfermline*	Henderson, Ebenezer, *The Annals of Dunfermline 1069–1878.* Glasgow, 1889.
Innes	Innes of Learney, Sir Thomas, *Scots Heraldry.* 2nd Edition. Edinburgh, 1956.
Jeffrey, *Roxburghshire*	Jeffrey, Alexander, *The History and Antiquities of Roxburghshire and Adjacent Districts.* 4 vols. Edinburgh, 1855–1864.
Harvey Johnston	Johnston, George Harvey, *The Heraldry of the Stewarts.* Edinburgh, 1906.
Kilgour, *Lochaber*	Kilgour, Wm. T., *Lochaber in War and Peace.* Paisley, 1908.
Laing, *i*	Laing, Henry, *Descriptive Catalogue of Impressions from Ancient Scottish Seals.* Edinburgh, 1850.
Macgeorge	Macgeorge, Andrew, *An Inquiry as to the Armorial Insignia of the City of Glasgow.* Glasgow, 1866.
Millar, *Cumbernauld*	Millar, Hugo B., *Historical Cumbernauld.* Cumbernauld, 1968.
Nisbet	Nisbet, Alexander, *A System of Heraldry.* New Edition. 2 vols. Edinburgh, 1816.
Old Edinburgh Club	*The Book of the Old Edinburgh Club.* Edinburgh, 1908–
Paul, *Scots Peerage*	*The Scots Peerage.* Edited by Sir James Balfour Paul. 9 vols. Edinburgh, 1904–1914.
Porteous	Porteous, Alexander, *The Town Council Seals of Scotland.* Edinburgh, 1906.
Pryde	Pryde, George Smith, *The Burghs of Scotland.* Oxford, 1965.
PSAS	*Proceedings of the Society of Antiquaries of Scotland.* Edinburgh, 1851–1852–

Seton   Seton, George, *The Law and Practice of Heraldry in Scotland*. Edinburgh, 1863.

Storer Clouston, *Orkney*   Clouston, J. Storer, *A History of Orkney*. Kirkwall, 1932.

SW   Stevenson, J. H., Wood, Marguerite, *Scottish Heraldic Seals*. Glasgow, 1940.

Third Statistical Account, Lanark   *The Third Statistical Account of Scotland: The County of Lanark*. Edited by George Thomson. Glasgow, 1960.

Tullibardine   *A Military History of Perthshire 1660–1902*. Edited by Katharine, Marchioness of Tullibardine (later Duchess of Atholl). Perth, 1908.

Wilson, *Renfrewshire*   Wilson, John, *General View of the Agriculture of Renfrewshire*. Paisley, 1812.

REFERENCE NOTES

In addition to the references listed below, much of my information has been obtained from Lyon Office Case Files.

I. THE NEW COUNCILS AND THEIR HERALDRY

1 House of Commons Reports 1971–72, 828: 1477–1485.
2 Ibid., 1972–73, 858: 163–281; 861: 712–873; House of Lords Reports 1972–73, 344: 1017–1086.
3 The burghs illegally using arms in 1975 were Aberlour, Kingussie and Millport.
4 House of Lords Reports 1972–73, 344: 1087.
5 Innes, 223.
6 SW, i, 76 (provisionally 1378).
7 Nisbet, i, 136.

II. THE ARMS OF THE COUNCILS

2 Highland
Caithness
Sutherland
1 The district of Tongue & Farr, which was included in Caithness in Schedule 1 (Part III) to the Local Government (Scotland) Act 1973, was transferred back to Sutherland by the Boundaries Commission after an appeal to the Secretary of State.

Ross & Cromarty
2 SW, i, 57.

Lochaber
3 Kilgour, *Lochaber*, 107–108.

Inverness
4 SW, i, 66.

Badenoch & Strathspey
5 Pryde, 148.

Nairn
6 SW, i, 74.

3 Grampian
City of Aberdeen
1 SW, i, 52.
2 Cruickshank, 29, 41.
3 Seton, 511.

Kincardine & Deeside
4   Barron, *Regalia,* 21: the traditional version which accords a leading part to Mrs Grainger does not seem to be well-founded.

4   Tayside
Angus
1   Paul, *Scots Peerage,* i, 160, 167.

City of Dundee
2   SW, i, 59
3   Bute, *RPB,* 108

Perth & Kinross
4   Tullibardine, 200, 223, plate facing 136, plate facing 109
5   Nisbet, i, 61; Fox Davies, *Heraldry,* 339

5   Fife
Fife
1   Laing, *i,* 334
2   Burgoyne, 6 et seq.

Kirkcaldy
3   Porteous, 177
4   *Fife Advertiser,* 7 May 1927
5   Pryde, 113

North East Fife
6   Bute, *RPB,* 78
7   Bain, iii, 1652

Dunfermline
8   Henderson, *Dunfermline,* 145
9   Porteous, 102

6   Lothian
City of Edinburgh
1   SW, i, 61
2   *Old Edinburgh Club,* iii, 11: Paul, Sir James Balfour, *The Armorial Bearings of the City of Edinburgh*

Midlothian
3   Nisbet, i, 372
4   Ibid., i, 163

7   Central
Falkirk
1   Buchanan, *Scotland,* i, 23–24

8   Borders
Tweeddale
1   Buchan, *Peebles-shire,* iii, 377.

Ettrick & Lauderdale
2   Craig-Brown, *Selkirkshire,* ii, 150.

Roxburgh
3   Jeffrey, *Roxburghshire*, i, 44.

9   Strathclyde
Dumbarton
1   SW, i, 58.

City of Glasgow
2   Macgeorge, passim.

Clydebank
3   Pryde, 390.

Strathkelvin
4   Porteous, 180.

Cumbernauld & Kilsyth
5   Miller, Cumbernauld, 15, 45.

Hamilton
6   Pryde, 152.
7   *Third Statistical Account, Lanark*, 70.

Eastwood
8   Wilson, *Renfrewshire*, 117.

Lanark
9   *PSAS*, v, 153–159: *Reid, Thomas, The Seven Seals of Lanark*; Bain, iii, 1652

Cunninghame
10   Nisbet, i, 192.
11   SW, i, 67.
12   Fox-Davies, *Public Arms*, 838.

Kyle & Carrick
13   Laing *i*, 782; Harvey Johnston, 15.

10   Dumfries & Galloway
Nithsdale
1   SW, i, 58.
2   SW, i, 80.

11   Islands Areas
Orkney
1   Storer Clouston, *Orkney*, 375
2   *Orcadian*, 13 July 1978: *Crawford, Barbara, The Orkney Arms*.

Appendix II
Doune
1   Pryde, 287.

CARTOGRAPHIC UNIT
UNIVERSITY of SOUTHAMPTON

Stirling
Stirling
Alloa
Bearsden
& Milngavie
Cumbernauld &
Kilsyth
Dumbarton
Falkirk
Falkirk
Clydebank
Dumbarton
Strathkelvin
Greenock
Cumbernauld
Kirkintilloch
Inverclyde
Clydebank
Monklands
Bearsden
Paisley
Coatbridge
Glasgow
City of
Glasgow
Renfrew
Motherwell
Giffnock
Motherwell
Cunninghame
Eastwood
East
Kilbride
Hamilton
Hamilton
Lanark
Kilmarnock
& Loudoun
East
Kilbride
Irvine
Lanark
Kilmarnock
0 Miles 10
0 Km 20
ORKNEY
Kirkwall
Wick
SHETLAND
Lerwick
WESTERN ISLES
Stornoway
Caithness
Wick
Sutherland
Golspie
Ross & Cromarty
Dingwall
Elgin
Banff
Nairn
Moray
Banff & Buchan

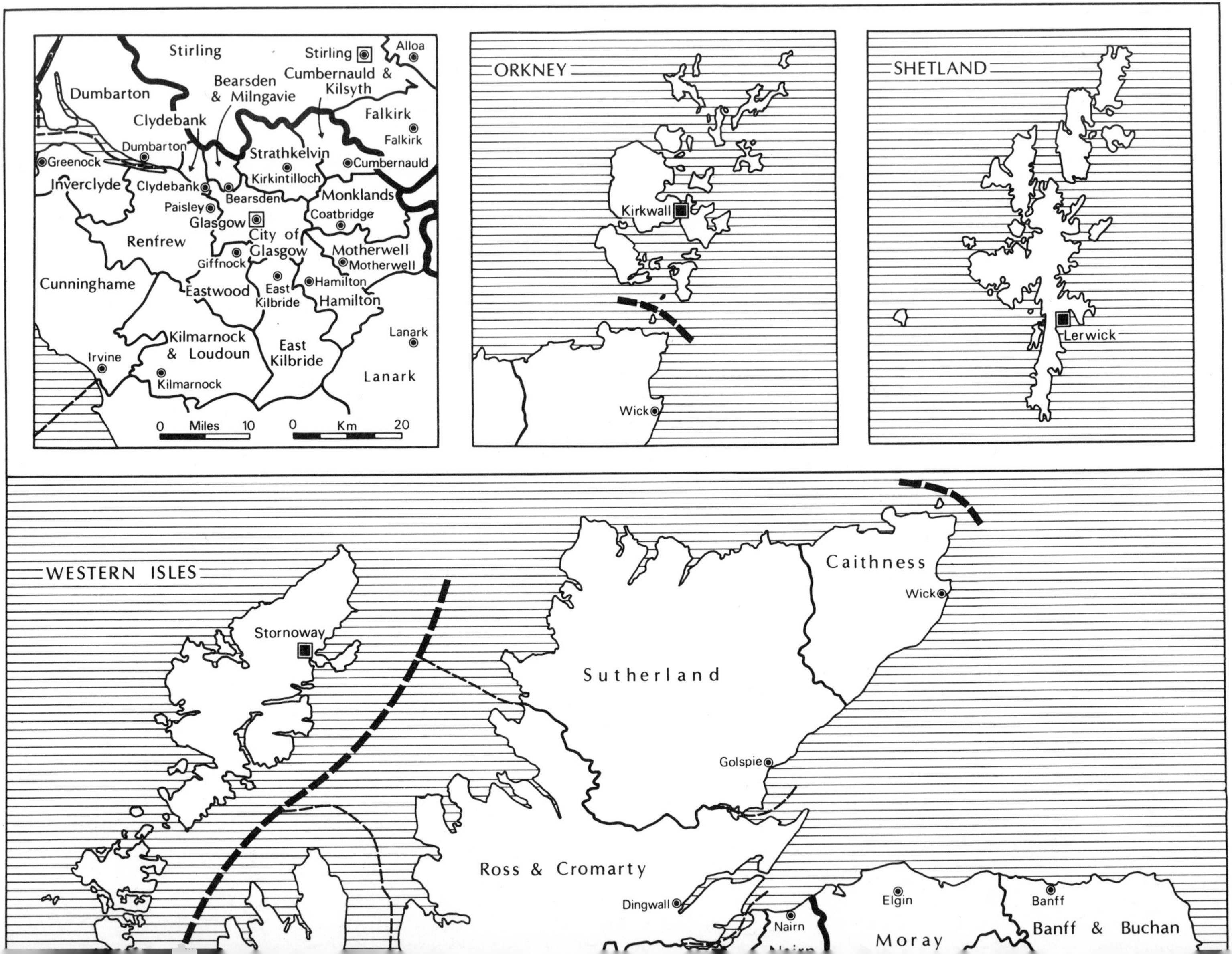

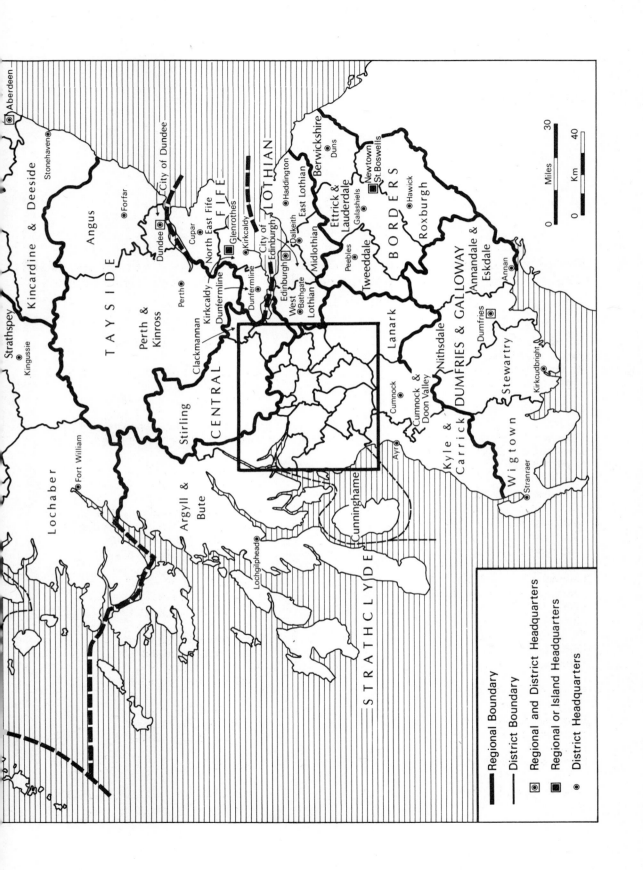

INDEX

This index contains only direct references to Council names. Regional and Islands Councils are shown in capitals; the entry relating to the main article about each Council is shown in bold type.